HOW TO TELL YOUR FAMILY THE TRUTH ABOUT THEIR
SPIRITUAL CAPTIVITY

Also available as eBook

AVAILABLE AT AMAZON.COM

By Lew White
VISIT AUTHOR'S PAGE AT AMAZON

Copyright © 2022 by Lew White

Published by Torah Institute
TORAHZONE.NET

Opening thoughts by the author:
"If pastors had been teaching the Ten Commandments that train us how to love, evolution and abortion would have never been issues to deal with. Instead, we hear them saying "don't be legalistic," and they quote dogmas promoting dispensational theology. Yahuah does not change."

TABLE OF CONTENTS

INTRODUCTION
Spiritual Captivity - How To Tell Your Family

Reading this book is like that scene in the Wizard Of Oz when Toto (the dog) pulls the cord and opens the curtain. This revealed the deception.

Culture shock happens to all who look behind the curtain and see the wizard for the first time.

If a person studies the **origins** of such things as Christmas, Easter, or Halloween, the superficial delusion of what we think they represent is exposed.

Once you've seen the other side of the cultural celebrations, the truth of how they became acceptable makes them impossible for a rational person to continue in.

The first response is to avoid talking about how and why we inherited the traditions.

Two cannot walk together unless they agree (Amus 3:3). Our society, parents, pastors, and educators pass on traditions camouflaged long ago to hide their pagan origins, mostly without knowing it.

When we learn the Truth, we become responsible to share it, not cover it with a basket.

When we share these things with loved ones, a defense mechanism immediately flares up, and they want to defend them. At that point, the hope having a rational discussion on the subject seems impossible.

This book is a bridge to help build a road of communication without friction.

The issues can be easily verified here in the Information Age, or continued to be blissfully ignored. Receiving a love of the Truth is a precious gift. Failing to share Truth with those who are perishing in their *spiritual captivity* carries heavy consequences (Ez. / Yeqezqal 33).

Blowing the shofar to warn them awakens them, and they can escape from their stronghold (prison).

"Teaching authorities don't teach, they control teachings, and those who think they're teachers."

2 Timothy 4:3-4:

"For there shall be a time when they shall not bear sound teaching, but according to their own desires, they shall heap up for themselves teachers tickling the ear, and they shall indeed turn their ears away from the Truth, and be turned aside to myths."

Adopted pagan symbols and behavior include:
Asherah trees, sacraments, holy water, transubstantiation, Sun-day, trinities, celibacy, image worship, popes, nuns, monks, monstrances, chants, special days adopted from heathens, lent, prayers to the dead, indulgences, purgatory, pilgrimages, stigmatas, steeples / pillars, Easter eggs, December 25th Solstice birth, the Greek *Olympic Games* dedicated to Zeus, their Sun deity, and uninspired words, traditions, and teachings]. Everything people enthusiastically celebrate comes to us from a tainted background.

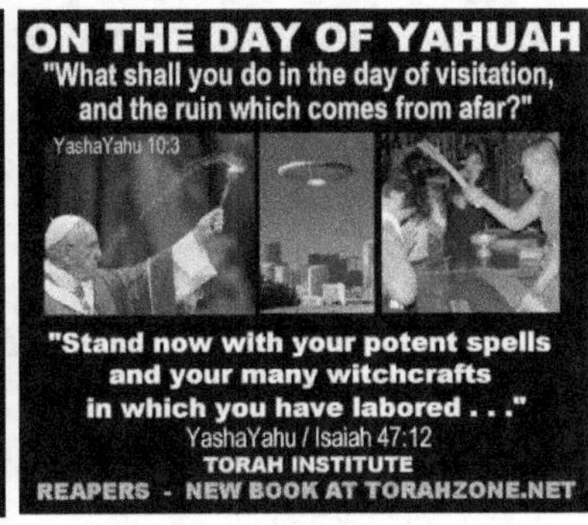

From infancy, we absorb information from family and teachers that amounts to fallacy and worthless traditions. This is verified by *YirmeYahu / Jer. 16:19.*
It's not just entertainment; there is a *diabolical plan* behind it all, and children are the primary target. The word **diabolical** literally means *"of DIABLOS"* – the Spanish word for *devil.*
A philosopher said,

"Give me the child for the first seven years and I'll give you the man." Originally spoken by Aristotle, this became a *Jesuit maxim* by Inigo Loyola S.J., the founder of the Order *Societas IESV.* In 1534, Loyola and six others met outside

Paris, France in a crypt beneath a church to pronounce specific vows, and absolute obedience to the pope.

The *Jesuit Order* was officially recognized as a new Order by pope Paul III by a papal bull titled **Regimini Militantis Ecclesiae** on September 27th, 1540.
It is a counter-reformation military organization, and considers its field of operation to be worldwide in scope. The linkage between the nobility and the clergy is clear. JFK opposed secret societies openly in his speeches. A few weeks after this photo was taken, he was assassinated.

This **secret society** has influenced governments and teaching institutions around the world. It was founded as a **military** organization to restore power to the papacy, and the members of the order refer to themselves as **soldiers** of the Roman Catholic church.

It is a *counter-reformation* organization, and has enormous influence in many other organizations, especially through the United Nations' initiatives. All forms of media and education have long been infiltrated by its operatives. This author was educated by these highly-skilled educators, yet escaped being overcome by the *"spiritual exercises"* they exerted.

The *fictions* people are taught, and grow up to **believe** from their youth, are passed into their offspring, and it continues until someone comes along to show them reality, and it is accepted. This book is one vehicle that will expose you to the Truth. If you accept it, the spell can be broken, and the **Truth** will set you free. Yahusha is the Truth.

Why People Find Truth To Be Disturbing At First
Consider the fact that the world economy is driven by a **pattern of celebrations** that cycle around every year.
The merchants' put up displays around these celebrations, and you see them everywhere you go, and one changes into another until they start again from the top.
These celebrations are all based on camouflaged pagan rituals that deal with *esoteric* (hidden) knowledge concerning fertility. It runs the gamut of all human history, yet unseen!

Think; the symbols people see have a message not perceived by the casual observer. *Eggs* and *rabbits* are right in your face, yet not perceived at first as being about **fecundity**. The trees, ornaments, tinsel, and wreaths are actual *sexually explicit components*, but may not be detected by an outside observer over their lifetime, until someone is sent to explain what they really represent. Every nuance of society is permeated with practicing **shameful idolatry**, and those who can overcome the pressures of family and friends and **escape** are regarded as betrayers, heretics, or under the influence of a *cult*. The whole world is in the power of the evil one, and through a network of spiritual principalities has trained all of civilization to be rebellious* against the Creator. There is a day appointed when all the world will be judged by one Man for their behavior, whether good or bad. That Man was raised from the dead as evidence of this fact (Acts 17). This may be the only warning you will ever hear, so please consider what you are about to read with thoughtfulness before you reject it. *rebelliousness is as witchcraft

"He who answers a matter before listening, it is folly and shameful to him." Proverbs 18:13

How can so many be ignorant? They are taught to dwell on folly, and they fall prey to men's philosophies and traditions.

Of all books printed in the world, the categories reveal a disinterest in the pursuit of Truth, and a love for futility:

Children's books: 46%
Fictional books: 39%
Religious books: 8%
Non-fiction books: 7%

Nonsense is perpetuated with the approval of all those immersed in it, including parents, teachers, pastors, and rulers at all levels. What you have not yet recognized as nonsense will amaze you because there is so much of it.

FICTIONAL CHRISTMAS
An Esoteric View Of The Mythological Christmas
What and Who It's Really About

December 25th has been someone's birthday for over 4000 years. He was the first king on Earth, built Babel, a tower, and became the first mighty-one; Nimrod, the god-man.
This rebel wanted to shoot an arrow at Yahuah from the top of the tower.
He founded the worship of the *host of heaven*, known today as **Astrology**.
This worship of the Mazzaroth or zodiac (animal-shaped star groups) is based on celebrating the re-birth of the Sun at the time of the winter solstice in December.
Since ancient times, the Solar birthday and all of the symbols associated with Sun worship were practices honoring the **deification of Nimrod**. Nimrod became the *template* for all Sun worship.
His name was babbled in the confusion of languages, becoming *Shammash, Ra, Mithras, Molok, Baal, Apollo, Kronos, Orion, Gott, Odin, Zeus, Krishna, etc.,*.
His identity is *occulted* in the character of Santa Claus / Krampus, or Old Nick.

PROGRAMMED FROM CHILDHOOD

The founder of the Societas Iesu used this maxim: ***"Give me the child for the first seven years and I'll give you the man."*** Inigo Loyola, founder of Societas IESV, or Jesuits.
A day is coming when all mankind will be judged for causing stumbling blocks, the main reason you are reading about it.

CHILDREN ARE THE TARGET

Maimonides (1135-1204) wrote about the the strong **opinion of habit** in his book,
<u>Guide For The Perplexed</u>:
"Men like the opinions to which they have been accustomed from their youth; they defend them, and shun contrary views; and this is one of the things that prevents men from finding truth, for they cling to the opinion of habit."
2Tim 4:4 says teachers will abandon the Truth and turn aside to myths.

MISSIONARY ADAPTATION OF CHRISTMAS

Dionysius Exiguus, a Scythian monk, visited Rome in the year 525. He witnessed Rome's fertility festival of Saturnalia, and was appalled by it.
History tells us he modified the reason for the celebration. The whole world now thinks of December 25th as the birth of Messiah, a revision mostly unexplored by most people. People live on lies and myths passed down.
Every popular celebration you can think of is directly inherited from pagan fertility worship from our ancestors. Paul was concerned that his work had been in vain among the Galatians. Being formerly heathens, they were falling back into their old pagan traditions, and "**special days**." He called their former pagan customs "weak and miserable principles."
Pastors falsely teach their flocks that these Galatians were falling back into Torah! Yahusha is opening our eyes now, and abiding in His Word is setting us free of the devil's schemes. He is calling us to **come out** of the mother of harlots (Babel's traditions). Even the word Easter refers to Ishtar; her Celtic name was Eostre. Her flower was the lily, and her Sun-spiked image stands in New York harbor.

Celebrating Christmas is adapted from Sun worship.
All pastors know it, but don't teach about it. They will defend the pagan origins, explaining how it doesn't matter because the **purpose** for it has been re-directed.
They react with the statement, **"It doesn't mean that anymore."** Some will confess that **everything** Christianity practices is inherited from pagans, verifying YirmeYahu (Jer.) 16:19. Sun worship literally transformed itself into the thousands of religious sects known by many names, hiding its origins from the ignorant masses by a policy of missionary adaptation, also known as: *syncretism*.
When we refuse to *receive a love for the Truth*, Yahuah sends us a strong delusion to believe the lie, 2 Thes. 2:11.

WHAT IS MISSIONARY ADAPTATION?

This a *teaching method* used to shape the existing beliefs, words, symbols, and practices of a *culture* into different meanings. This method served well to spread Catholicism. This behavior is still reinforced and condoned as doing a "greater good," but from the viewpoint of Yahuah it is a scheme of the devil to teach the traditions of men as a form of righteousness, while abandoning the Word of Yahuah. (see 2Tim. 3). Borrowing the habits of other cultures, especially their religious ones and blending them, is also known as **syncretism**. Pastors know this, but allow people to keep following the broad road to destruction.

Another warning about *turning aside to myths* is recorded at 2 Tim. 4. Peter tells how the false teachers would be saying the **Truth is evil** at 2 PETER 2:1-3:

"But there also came to be false prophets among the people, as also among you there shall be false teachers, who shall secretly bring in destructive heresies, and deny the Master Who bought them, bringing swift destruction on themselves. And many shall follow their destructive ways, because of whom the way of Truth shall be evil spoken of, and in greed, with fabricated words, they shall use you for gain. From of old their judgment does not linger, and their destruction does not slumber."

Those teaching the Truth in the last days are exposing the schemes of the devil, getting the bride cleaned-up.

WEAK AND MISERABLE PRINCIPLES

Christmas, birthdays, Easter, and Halloween are "**special days**" in the eyes of most people, and entwined very strongly with family bonds.

Yahuah forbids us to mimic pagans.

We've been duped, and witchcraft has entangled itself with our family bonds. When we abandon pagan customs and explain why we can no longer practice them, we are accused of being hateful, *and they heap abuse on us.*

1 Peter 4 shows us what's happening:
"Consequently, he does not live out his remaining time on earth for human passions, but for the will of Alahim. For you have spent enough time in the past carrying out the same desires as the pagans: living in debauchery, lust, drunkenness, orgies, carousing, and detestable idolatry. Because of this, they consider it strange of you not to plunge with them into the same flood of reckless indiscretion, and they heap abuse on you...."

This is what Yahuah means about us being the salt of the Earth: **If we live among them and they hardly notice us, we have lost our saltiness.**
At Rev. 12 Yahusha describes for us a great sign: the *"woman clothed with the Sun"* with the Moon under her feet is His own unwary bride, surrounded by the 12 star patterns. **She is defiled by all her idolatrous Sun worship.** Our acts of obedience are our white robes. We no longer walk as pagans.

"Come out of her!" (Rev. 18:4) Yahusha uses these words to call His bride out of the teachings of the harlot mother *before releasing His wrath*.
See Mt. 24 and YashaYahu / Isaiah 24.

WHEN WAS YAHUSHA BORN?
Tradition informs us Yahusha (Jesus) was born Dec. 25th (Christmas Day), and shepherds and Magi came that night to worship the Child. The Truth is far different in practically every detail.
To the Romans, December 25 was the time of *Saturnalia*, celebrated with wild frivolity, drunken feasting, and fertility symbols to herald the re-birth of their Sun deity, Apollo.
All Sun deities are Nimrod babbled in other names. Soldiers knew him as the Persian form, **Mithras**, the slayer of the bull (the zodiac / animal constellation, Taurus.

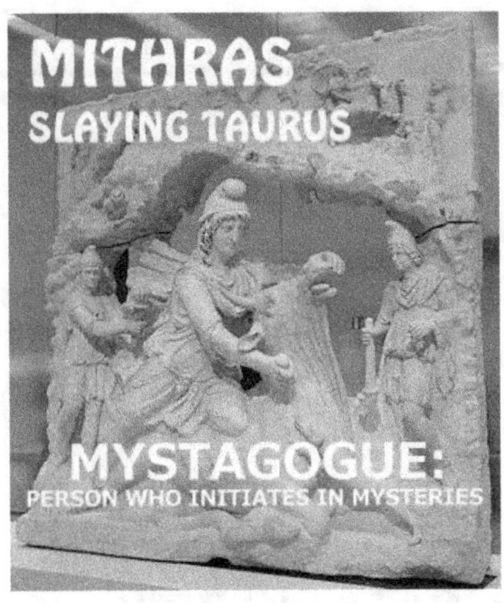

This figure is located at the Vatican. See the hat of Mithras and the elves on the right and left? These clues show us we're looking at *Santa*, an esoteric Nimrod Solar diety. Dec. 25th was adopted to revise the pagan festival into a Christian festival. In 321, Constantine enforced Rome's *venerable day of the Sun*, replacing the 7th day Shabath as a day to rest.

Sunday is not Yahuah's Shabath. Hebrews 4 proves it. Occult practices were camouflaged with new interpretations, leaving the symbols and behavior perfectly intact to this day. Mithras was the Persian Sun deity popularized by the Roman soldiers. They went *full-tilt Nimrod* too.

CHRISTMAS: A SATANIC PRACTICE
A 17th century Puritan Public Notice:
"The observance of Christmas having been deemed a sacrilege, the exchanging of gifts and greeting, dressing in fine clothing, feasting and similar satanical practices are hereby forbidden, with the offender liable to a fine of five shillings."

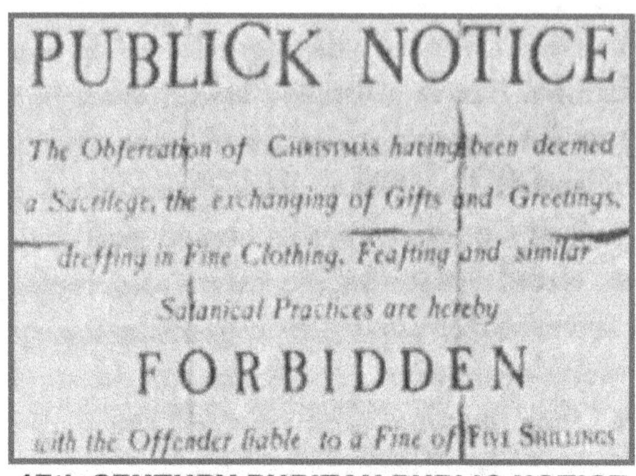

17th CENTURY PURITAN PUBLIC NOTICE

CHRISTMAS
A SATANIC PRACTICE

SANTA IS THE NIMROD SUN DEITY

The Sun's birthday has been celebrated for 4000 years on the same day.

Santa Claus is a mispronunciation of saint Nicholas, heard in English as **SANTICLAUS**.

Saint Nicholas never existed, but is a Catholic myth.

The world is deluded by similar myths.

The Celtic word for "child feast" is YULE.

The *yule log* is related to Nimrod as the Sun deity, bringing back light and warmth to the world. His birthday, and other kings after him, were the earliest form of birthday celebrations. Most of the world goes by a calendar year heavily influenced by this ancient association with the king's birthday. Nimrod is all over this, and his mythology hovers near the fireplace of homes today as families burn a *yule log* in the hope of his arrival down the chimney.

In the Celtic (Druid) tongue, Yule means *child*.

To these heathens, **yuletide** meant a death, not a birth.

A child was offered to their Sun deity.

The **fireplace** was a Roman family's worship place.

The most important day to a witch is their own birthday.

The custom to surround oneself with loved ones on this day is believed to protect the celebrant from evil.

Witches worship **mother nature**, their "goddess."

The Norse **Ostara** is the old term for Babel's Ishtar, the Earth mother, also known widely now as **Easter**.
We have inherited ***nothing*** but futility, and pastors declare Yahuah's Word is *done away*. Most live as if they are pleasing Yahuah with their pagan behavior, as if He now loves the things He once called ***abominations***.
Nimrod's rebellion is also expressed in Humanism, encouraging people to serve Humanity rather than Yahuah.
Nimrod's objectives are reflected in the rising world order.
The man who invented Christmas was Nimrod; it is no coincidence that his avatar-deities (which exist only in the imaginations of men) were all supposedly born on December 25th:
Mithras, Helios, Horus, Attis, Zeus, Dionysus (son of Zeus)**, Jupiter, Ra, Perseus, Tammuz, Hercules, Baal, Bacchus, Apollo, Molok, Sol, Inti, Krishna, Jahbulon, Odin / Woden, Surya, and Baphomet.**
The Scriptural directives and calendar were disregarded, and the framework of paganism was adopted, causing great confusion. Sun worship became disguised as ***Christianity***, *keeping every habit ever practiced by pagans:*
Sunday, holy water, statues, crosses, trees, wreaths, relics, rosaries, pillars, circumambulation, priestly vestments, scarves, talismans, domes, etc.,.
Danial 12:4 tells us in the end times **knowledge** (of Truth) **will increase.**
The neglected Scriptural festivals are **shadows** forming the **redemption plan**, and one of them foreshadows Sukkoth, or Tabernacles. (MARRIAGE SUPPER)
Those who practice idolatry will *not* be counted in the assembly at the marriage supper of the Lamb.
See Revelation 22:14-15.
Yahusha has ***never*** had anything to do with Christmas or December 25th; men forced this upon the ignorance masses.
Here in the *Information Age* ignorance is a choice. We can serve the traditions and commandments of men through recycled fertility festivals inherited from pagans, or we can wake up and serve the Creator of all things, our Redeemer ***Yahusha***.

Noah seemed to be a nutcase to the people of his time, until it started to rain. Look closely at the pictures above.
Sun worship involved child sacrifices. The dragon gave them their throne, or seat of authority.

Old Nick is a euphemism for the devil. Learn what a **Christmas tree** really is: it's an **ASHERAH.**
Asherim is the plural form, and is translated "groves" in the KJV. These trees are fertility objects formerly brought into homes and decorated by pagans (YirmeYahu / Jer 10).
Wreaths were placed on doors, and symbolize the birth canal at the time of the re-birth of the Sun at Dec. 25ᵗʰ.

"Perfect people are hard to get along with."
(quote by Sylvia Fashant, July 6, 2022).
There is only one exception we should recognize;
His Name is Yahusha ha Mashiak.
Google: YAHUSHA, and obey Him.
Watch what happens to you on the inside.

IS OBEDIENCE NOW HERESY?
Since the 4th century CE, Natsarim have been accused of being Judaizers, legalists, as well as shunning *"ecclesiastical powers / authorities."*

Our families trample our words because a prophet is not without honor *except* in his hometown (Mark 6:4).
Most people brush-off the Truth when they hear it because it conflicts with their perception of reality. They show us their disinterest and aggravation when we give them the Words of Yahusha. In these situations, the best approach is to *live* the Living Words so our example sends the message without speaking the words. The pastors have trained the whole world to disregard **obedience**, yet that is the only way our belief is perfected. Instead of obedience, the pastors teach the world how to sin with a seared conscience. The serpent has deceived the whole world through masquerading messengers of light, and it takes Yahusha to call us out of the **delusion**.
The **mind** (perspective) **of the flesh** does not want to obey, nor does it have the capacity to be able to obey.
The **Mind of the Ruach of Yahusha** gives us the ability to discern the philosophical schemes, so we are no longer a prey to be overcome by them. Without obedience, the objective of our belief, it is impossible to please Yahusha. *He only gives His Ruach to those who obey* Him (Acts 5:32).

HOW TO TELL YOUR FAMILY

We see it, but those living by the worldly pattern do not yet know they have been made drunk. Revelation 17:4-5 tells us all about the woman of Babel that made the world drunk on the abominations they do not yet perceive.
Your family and friends have noticed a **change** in you. There is a calm kindness they never saw before, and from their point-of-view, your enthusiasm for their yearly celebrations has completely dried-up. You now see the celebrations for what they really are.
You are like a foreigner to them now, and they do not understand you at all. Why are we perceiving things differently now? We have been given a new perspective: The MIND of the Ruach of Yahuah now dwells in us.
What changed, and why?
Our **obedience** changes everything. When we **obey** the eternal Covenant, we perfect and confirm our belief. We then receive the help of Yahusha indwelling us, but until we obey,

He will not give us His Ruach (Acts 5:32).

When you explain how you now desire to please Yahusha and walk in obedience and truth, their first impression is you have joined a cult. They wonder what kind of religious fanatics you've been fraternizing with.
Because the world is drunk on the wine (teachings) of the woman holding the golden cup of her abominations, Natsarim can expect to be hated because we follow Yahusha's Ten Words of love, rather than the traditions of men. The Word of Truth has renewed our minds, and we have awakened to the lies and schemes of the devil.

KOLOSSIANS 2:6-10
"See to it that no one makes a prey of you through philosophy and empty deceit, according to the tradition of men, according to the elementary things of the world, and not according to Mashiak. Because in Him dwells all the Fullness of Yahuah bodily, and you have been made complete in Him, who is the Head of all principality and authority."

LET'S START WITH THE REAL NAME
Proverbs 30:4 asks an important question:
"What is His Name, and what is His Son's Name, if you know it?"

Let's Pretend everyone has always known Yahusha's Real Name. In this world, people may use one of their other names, such as a *middle* name. Some use nicknames or professional brand-names like *Bono* or *Sting*.
When Jorge Mario Bergoglio was elected pope by the Cardinal electors in March 2013, he adopted the name *Francis*. Recently I asked a Catholic if they had ever heard of the name *Jorge Bergoglio*, and they said they had not.
Fake names happen for a variety of reasons.
Can we presume to refer to the Supreme Being by whatever name we choose?
Should we *allow teaching authorities* to continue molesting the **Name above all names?** People may be living in a false reality, *and never know it*. When they encounter the Truth,

the first reaction is to say, *"ridiculous!"* This experience is a form of stress called ***"cognitive disonnance."***
While we are pretending, imagine that everyone was suddenly told they were to never use the real Name **Yahusha**, but rather to always call Him **JESUS,** going forward. This is an example of what it seems like to your family, only the reverse is happening.
Truth is rejected to maintain traditions.
What would you do, knowing He never told us to do such a thing, but warned that this would actually happen:
"I have come in My Father's Name and you do not receive Me, if another comes in his own name, him you would receive. How are you able to believe, when you are receiving esteem from one another, and the esteem that is from the only Alahim you do not seek?"
Yahukanon / Jn. 5:43-44
Let's stop pretending as children, and come into reality concerning the real and only Name, **YAHUSHA**.

In the photo above we see an object called a *monstrance*. It's an object designed to hold a round piece of bread so people can kneel before it in worship. It is intentionally designed to cause people to violate the 1st, 2nd, and 3rd Commandments.

People don't know what they don't know.
People have to struggle to find someone to explain the message in the ***Writings of Truth*** (Danial 10:21).
Instead of teaching what the Word itself directs us to do, the people are directed away from it, and taught traditions.
The search for Truth is the pursuit to know our Creator.
Those who teach us lead us only into confusion.
The translations will show you in the preface there is an intentional attack on the Truth. The translators adopted a device to replace the Name of the Creator with "LORD."
LORD is the definition of the Hebrew word BAAL (BEL).
We will look at this in greater detail a little later.

Yahusha's greatest problem with the teachers was how they placed their *traditions* above Torah.
We must test everything we hear by the Word of Yahuah, and throw out the leaven of men's teachings.
Yahusha is our <u>only</u> Chief (Rabbi).

2 Thess 2:7-12 says there is delusion, and the deceptions will increase lawlessness, a working of error. Our teachers are the source of the error:

*"**For the mystery of lawlessness** (living without law) **is already at work; only he who now restrains** (controls) **will do so until he is taken out of the way. And then the lawless one will be revealed, whom the Master will consume with the breath of His mouth and destroy with the brightness of His coming.***
The coming of the lawless one is according to the working of satan, with all power, signs, and lying wonders, and with all unrighteous deception among those who perish, because they did not receive the love of the Truth that they might be saved. And for this reason Alahim will send them strong delusion, that they should believe the lie, that they all may be condemned

who did not believe the Truth but had pleasure in unrighteousness."
Take this book, and go ask your Christian pastor,
Do you teach Truth, or Tradition?

Scripture is loaded with warnings on how men will turn aside to myths and abandon sound teachings - 2Tim 4:4. All Scripture is Alahim-breathed and useful for teaching, rebuking, correcting, and training. 3:16-17.

Rev 12:17 reveals how those who guard the Commandments of Alahim and hold to the testimony of Yahusha enrage the dragon.
WHO ARE THE NICOLAITANES?
The word is used twice at Revelation 2, and is a term meaning **"rulers over the people."**
The traditions of men have replaced the ways of Yahuah with <u>**all**</u> the trappings of Sun worship.
The sickness is incurable. Yahusha is about to sweep away the *refuge of lies*, and pour out His Spirit on all flesh.
Pastors must be presented with these big questions so they can *turn away from their weak and miserable principles.*
They have excused and adopted *every* pagan tradition known, *and devoured the sheep they were entrusted to teach.* Yahusha's **Natsarim** are here to nourish and protect the sheep.
Be courageous but kind.
Ask these questions of your pastor:

Do you teach Truth?
What is the Renewed Covenant? *Jer. 31:31

Why does Christianity look exactly like Sun Worship? *Jer. = YIRMEYAHU [NO J IN HEBREW]
Is Scripture the Alahim-breathed Word of Yahuah, should all men live by it, and if they do, who will be offended the most?

Is Greek, or Hebrew, the more trusted source for Truth?
Why does everything seem to be derived from Greek?
Are sacraments real, or illusions?

Why do we meet in the morning on the first day of the week?

Should we be observing the festivals of Lev. 23?
Zek 14:16

Which festivals did Yahusha guard?

Were the festivals weak and miserable?

What is the Key of Knowledge?

Did Yahuah's Name become concealed by translators by the terms Adonai, Kurios, Dominus, then LORD?
                              Is He glad about it?

Is the name *JESUS* inspired, or an invention?
What does it mean, and why?
In Hebrew, it's "the horse," *HE SOOS.*
Why is the Name Yahusha *unknown*, and substituted?
Is the true Name important?
Does Yahusha mean *I am your Deliverer*?

Why are the 10 Commandments mostly ignored?

Can we build steeples knowing they are forbidden?
Lev. 26:1

Why does the state reward religious organizations tax exempt status?

Is the 501c3 status preventing clergy from teaching Yahuah's instructions condemning sexual contact between males or interspecies? Lev. 20:13

Is it still an abomination if a man lies with another man as if he were a woman?

If Torah is against an unborn child being hurt by accident, can it be assumed that Yahuah doesn't mind if someone kills an unborn child intentionally? Ex. 21:22-25

What relationship is there between the Sunday morning meetings, the state, and grocery stores selling beer?

Will there be Sunday morning meetings at steeples after Yahusha returns? Will there be wine at our marriage supper? Mt. 26:29

Did Yahusha drink wine? Did Paul advise Timothy to use wine to calm himself? 1Tim 5:23

At Ex. 30:23, is Kannabosim (Latin, Cannabis) **a primary ingredient in the anointing oil?**

Why don't we guard the 7th day rest (sign of the everlasting Covenant) **the Shabath, which Hebrews 4 says remains a rest for us? Should we do, or just hear the Word?**

What did Yahuah tell us is the reason He is coming to burn the Earth? YashaYahu / Is, 24:5
Why do Christians eat pigs? Is it because they misunderstood Peter's vision? Acts 10
How will pig-eaters be dealt with by Yahuah on the Day of Yahuah, according to YashaYahu / Isaiah 66?

Why do we decorate with pagan fertility symbols and celebrate pagan festivals and call them by different names?

What is the message of AliYah, and why haven't you warned us about it? Mal. 4:1-6

Why is behavior tightly controlled and never anything like Yahusha lived? 1Yn. 2:6 **Should we be concerned?**

What is sin? *Do you teach against it?* 1Yn. 3:4

What is repentance?
How do we acquire eternal life, and can it be done by continuing to sin?

If we pray repetitive prayers, or speak to the dead like Catholics, Muslims, and Hindus, does Yahusha hear us?

Is "holy water" derived from a Hindu ritual involving the Ganges River?

Where does Yahuah tell us He is 3 persons in one "GOD?" PAGAN: BAAL SHALISHI - 2KINGS 4:42
How many pagan cultures have trinities and use cross symbols to represent the Sun?

Why did the Latin Vulgate use *CRUX* **to translate** *stauros* (stake) **and not the Latin word** *stauro*?

Is Yahusha two persons, or is Yahusha the exact representation of Yahuah as Hebrews 1, Kol. 2:9, Phil. 2:11, Yn. 14:9, tell us? Why did they try to stone Yahusha at Yn. 10:33?

What is necromancy? Is a rosary different from a Ouija board? Are demons behind both?

How can we ignore Yahuah's Torah and still believe He hears our prayers, when He says He does not?
Proverbs 28:9

Is Astrology acceptable, and is it related to baking cakes, blowing out candles, making wishes to genies, & Nimrod's rebellion?

Is December 25th Yahusha's date of birth?
Did the magi visit Him with gifts then, or 2 years later?

Have we turned aside to any myths you can recognize?
Can you evaluate and recognize disobedience?

Is the word *EASTER** **the name of the mother of harlots, or should the KJV keep it at Acts 12:4 and strike the word Passover the other 28 times it is translated from the word** *PASCHA*? **Ishtar, Eostre, Asherah*
Is the KJV based on the *Latin Vulgate*, **and was it translated by Anglican Catholics? Was King James baptized as a baby in a Catholic circus?**
Can we pour hot coals into our laps and not be burned? Prov. 6:27

How will pig eaters stand on the great and awesome day of Yahuah? Is. / YashaYahu 66:17

Do you obey any of Yahuah's Commands?

If we teach and obey His Commandments, will He condemn us for it, like men do?

Can we obey the teachings of men, and obey the teachings of Yahuah also?
If not, which of the two should we obey?

Is being legal a good or bad thing to Him?

What makes *legalism* so detestable to so many pastors, and why does the word sound so toxic when spoken by most teachers? Is a legalist a heretic of some kind?
Where is the word "legalism" found in Scripture?

At Yn. 14:15, He said,
"If you love Me, guard My Commandments."
If we obey His Torah, are we trying to earn anything, or show Him we love Him?

If we believe only, and do not obey, *don't the demons do the same?*
If I have come to love Yahuah's Commandments, does that mean I'm doomed, or rather circumcised in my heart by Yahusha? Ez. 36:27, Jer. 31:31

Can we call on whatever name we want, or should we investigate what Scripture tells us is His true and only Hebrew Name?

For what reason is the dragon enraged at the seed of the woman? Rev. 12:17
If we abide in His Word, will we disappoint Yahusha, or the dragon?

What is Truth? Yn. 18:38
How can we know the Truth? Yn. 8:31, 32
What does the Truth set us free from?
Are the teaching authorities of men leading us into Truth, or the broad road to death?

<u>Go</u> to the pastors and show them the *traditions of men* have caused their *loss of saltiness.*

These questions have obvious answers, and anyone wielding the sword of Truth can shred the cardboard lies of the dragon.

The dragon is afraid because we <u>will</u> use the Sword on him. Paul explains how our weapons are not fleshly:

"For though we walk in the flesh, we do not fight according to the flesh. For the weapons we fight with are not fleshly but mighty in Yahuah for overthrowing strongholds, overthrowing reasonings and every high thing that exalts itself against the knowledge of Yahuah, taking captive every thought to make it obedient to the Mashiak, and being ready to evaluate all disobedience, when your obedience is accomplished."
2 Korinthians 10:3-6 **BYNV**

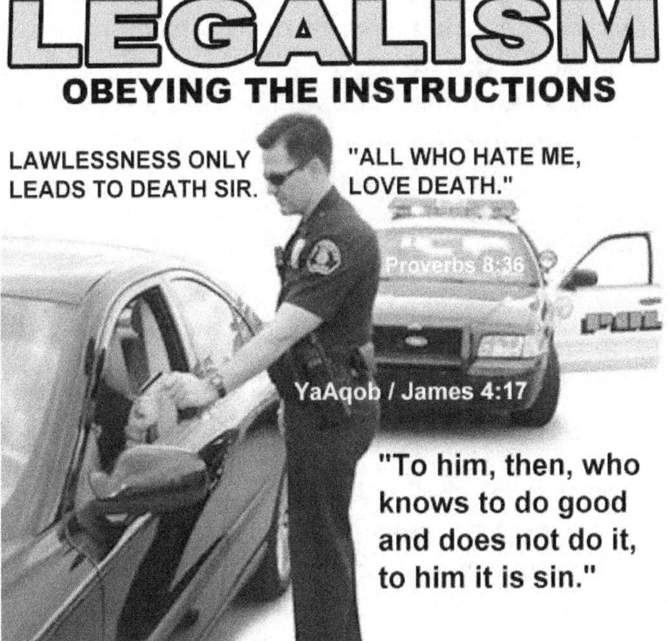

Yahusha's **yoke** (teaching) is easy, and it is His will that none perish, but rather that all come to repentance. He said, "Repent, or perish."

Our mission is to warn all mankind to repent, and obey.

Teach all nations to obey **everything** Yahusha commanded us. There is one Torah for the native-born and the foreigner who joins himself to Yahuah. Just as the first assembly in the wilderness was comprised of a mixed multitude of peoples, here in the last days the message of deliverance is being sent into all the nations. The Torah of kindness excludes no one from joining Yahuah through His Covenant, and foreigners are especially precious to Him (see YashaYahu / Is. 56). All who guard His Shabath are welcomed by Yahuah. **Foreigners** will be given a name **better** than sons and daughters. The sons and daughters are His cultivated fig tree and love the grafted-in branches, all sharing in the life of the **Root**.

Acts 17:30-31: **"Although Alahim overlooked the ignorance of earlier times, He now commands all men everywhere to repent. For He has set a DAY when He will judge the world with justice by the Man He has appointed. He has given proof of this to all men by raising Him from the dead."**

The hoards are taught to come to the steeples on their **SUN-days** to **worship** the *LORD*, hoping somehow someone will explain what Yahuah's Word means. Yahuah told us what day is **Shabath**, and not to go out of our place on the seventh day (Ex. 16:29). We are to **rest** in all our dwellings. ***Obedience is worship.***

Our teachers are the source of our error:
"For the leaders of this people lead them astray, and those who are guided by them are in confusion."
YashaYahu / Is. 9:16
Yahuah told us His **mark** is **His Shabath, a sign forever between Him and His people.**(Ex. 31:17) Our bond with Him is not a shade of skin or a denomination.
Our bond is ***Yahusha in us***. Kol. 1, Eph. 3, and Acts 5:32. Teachers are causing disobedience, divisions, and hatred, missing the goal of love, **"desiring to be teachers of Torah, but they do not understand what they are saying or that which they so confidently affirm."**

1Tim 1:7 shows us how the blind guides have distorted the message, and heaped-up teachers to say what itching ears desire to hear. The way of Truth has been maligned as evil. 2 Peter 2:2

Only the Aharonic Covenant is obsolete now.

The *Everlasting Covenant* is written on our hearts.

This is the circumcision of the heart done by the Spirit of Yahusha, and we receive a love for the Truth, His Word. We're scattered into the nations because we would not obey His Covenant of love, and He is about to re-gather us from the ends of the Earth (Dt. 4). He is calling for many hunters and fishers to train a remnant of obedient workers to warn mankind to be **restored to favor**, and sealing us as His property. (Ps. 91, Is. 7:18-25, Yual 2, 1Thess. 5, and hundreds of other repeated warnings)

If teachers do not **teach** Yahuah's Torah, then **"there is no light in them."** Is. 8:20

Another question may help awaken a pastor:
What will it cost you as a pastor if you teach your assembly the Truth instead of **traditions**?
What will it cost you if don't, and keep telling them the lies our fathers have handed-down to us?

Jeremiah / YirmeYahu 16:19:
"O Yahuah, my strength and my stronghold, and my refuge in the DAY OF DISTRESS; To You the nations will come from the ends of the Earth and say, "Our fathers have inherited NOTHING but lies, futility, and things of no profit."

Learn what <u>He</u> likes, not <u>men</u> - Eph. 5:10

"Have I now become your enemy by telling you the Truth? - Gal. 4:16 *Who has deceived you?*

Remember, Paul was concerned his labors were in vain among the Galatians because they were falling back into their former pagan days, months, and years.

These were *their* former "weak and miserable principles" he referred to at Galatians 4:9, not Yahuah's Torah.

Rev. 18:3: "All the nations drunk the wine of the passion of her immorality. The kings of the Earth were immoral with her, and the merchants of the Earth have grown wealthy through the extravagance of her luxury."

All the **fertility practices** have made the merchants wealthy: birthdays, Christmas, Easter, Valentines, Halloween; and now you must decide who you will serve.

YOU ARE THE SERVANT OF THE ONE YOU OBEY
Romans 6:16

Woe to those who mislead one of His little ones.

Knowing the elements will melt with intense heat, what sort of people ought you to be? Join us, be restored to favor.

UNINSPIRED WORDS & TRADITIONS

Get Wisdom

All the pillars, obelisks, and steeples come from the cup held by the **whore of Babel**. She has made all the nations drunk from the filth of her abominations. We are not to learn the ways of the nations.
"Do not make idols for yourselves, and do not set up a carved image or a pillar for yourselves, and do not place a stone image in your land, to bow down to it. For I am Yahuah your Alahim." Lev. 26

Danial described the end of days, and Yahusha also spoke of him, and a time of the great distress of nations:

"And those who have insight shall shine like the brightness of space, and those who lead many to obedience like the stars forever and ever. But you, Danial, hide the words; seal the book until the time of the end. Many shall diligently search and knowledge shall increase." Danial 12:3-4 - *look at this:*

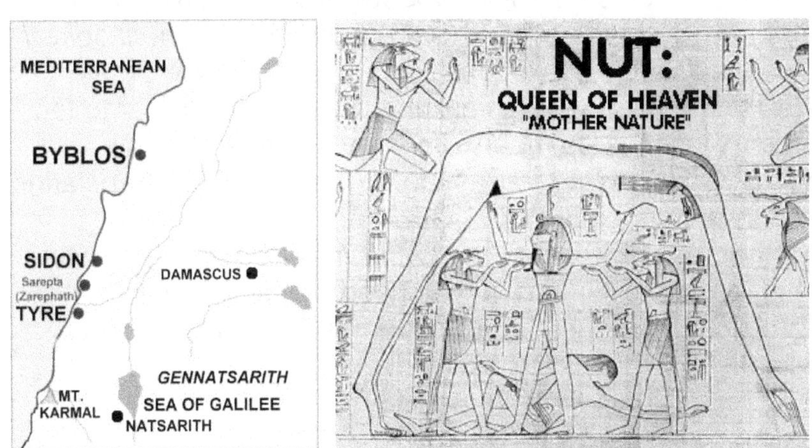

World History Encyclopedia:

*"***Byblos*** was the ancient port city of Gebal (called *Byblos* by the Greeks) on the coast of the Mediterranean sea in what is today Lebanon. Pagan temples were located in coastal ports to exploit sexual tourism. Worship of the zodiac (host of heaven) in their services was sexual, and this produced an overflow of unwanted children. *Infanticide* was the sacrificing of the children we read about at Lev. 18. Today we hear teachers refer to the *Bible*,
a word originating from one of these fertility deities. Byblos is the name for one coastal city.
Because papyrus was one of the principal articles in its trade, the Greeks took the *name of the city* as their word for book - ***biblos*** – and from their word for books named our Bible - *ta biblia* - which means *'the books'."*
The temple of Byblia gave the city its name, and also the book now referred to as the Bible. It is <u>uninspired</u>!
Another source says,
*"Both the city of Byblos in ***Phoenicia*** and the city Byblis in ***Egypt*** were named after the female deity Byblis (also called Byble or Biblis). This idol was the grand-daughter of Apollo,*

the Greek pagan sun-idol.
Byblia *was also a name for* ***Venus****, an astral goddess and a goddess of sensuality among the ancient Greeks."*
When asked if the word ***Bible*** *is a pagan word, organizations that use the word Bible in their name claim it is not a problem, but comes to us from the word for paper or parchment in the Greek language. In other words, "nothing here, move along." Bible is not a word used in the inspired text.* The ***inspired*** text calls itself
KETHAB AMATH at Danial 10:21. See an interlinear to fact check; these words mean *Writing of Truth* in Hebrew.
We have grown far too trusting. Eusebius began translating the Greek into Latin in 391 CE.
For the next 1200 years his *Latin Vulgaris (common)* was believed to be inspired. It was used by the Anglican Catholics to produce the King James Version.

SEAPORT CITIES offered easy access for wealthy traders to sell and buy all kinds of goods.
The pagan temples located in these ports exploited the rich travelers tourism with brothels.
The fertility temples' reference, ***worship services****,* is still used commonly by gentile cultures.

Shrine prostitutes brought great wealth to the cities through their shameful deeds. Paul warned his converts, who had once been in these *worship services*: ***"And have no fellowship with the fruitless works of darkness, but rather expose them. For it is a shame even to speak of what is done by them in secret.***
But all things being exposed are manifested by the light, for whatever is manifested is light." - Ephesians 5:11-13
We must not learn the ways of the heathen (Dt. 18).

See Dt. 18, 2 Kings 16, 17, 21, YirmeYahu 32

Infanticide was institutionalized to eradicate surplus babies the ***fertility rites*** produced. Unwanted children were burned in the belly of Molok, a metal furnace in the form of an idol. Drums, trumpets, bells, shakers, and rattles were used to create a great din to cover the dying screams of the infants being burned alive. **Abortion** is today's Molok worship.

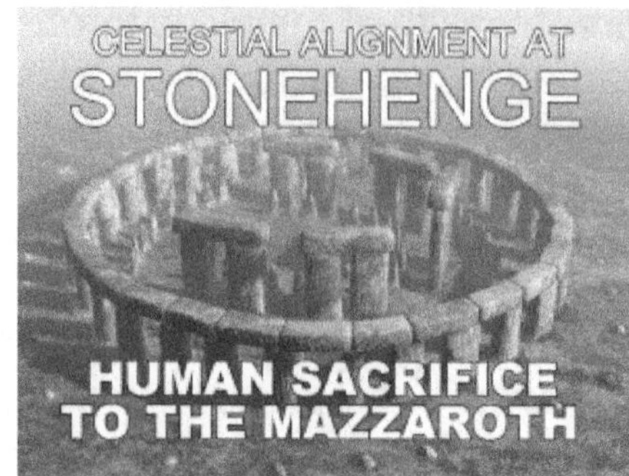

Yahuah is going to burn the inhabitants of the Earth (YashaYahu 24)

JESUS: *Uninspired Word*

A word of recent origin, Jesus is less than 500 years old.
The letter J was invented from the Greek letter IOTA.
It grew a curly tail in the 17th century when used as the first
letter in a sentence, or the first letter of a proper noun.
The *Latin Vulgate*, and the 1st edition of the KJV used **IESV**
to represent the Name, and had never known the true Name,
YAHUSHA.
1 Korinthians 12:2 reminds us:
*"You know that you were **guyim**, led away to the dumb idols,
even as you might be led."*
In this case, guyim is a reference to the nations, idolaters,
and all foreigners living outside the Covenant.
By using the word *BIBLE*, the Word of Yahuah is being
referred to by the actual name originating from a female idol
of pleasure worshiped in Canaan & Egypt.

WHO IS *"THE LORD GOD?"*

Read your translations' **Preface**. It admits removing the
Name of YAHUAH, and replacing it with a device;
the English word **LORD**.
Confute the *uninspired* words.
The name GOD was adopted by Christianity as was BIBLE:

**"GOD (god) Common Teutonic word for personal object
of religious worship, formerly applicable to super-
human beings of heathen myth; on conversion of
Teutonic races to Christianity, term was applied to
Supreme Being."** - *1945 Encyclopedia Americana*

Exodus 23:13: ***"And in all that I have said to you take heed. And make no mention of the names of other mighty ones, let it not be heard from your mouth."***

Let's prove what we claim to believe, and live by every word that proceeds from the mouth of Yahuah.

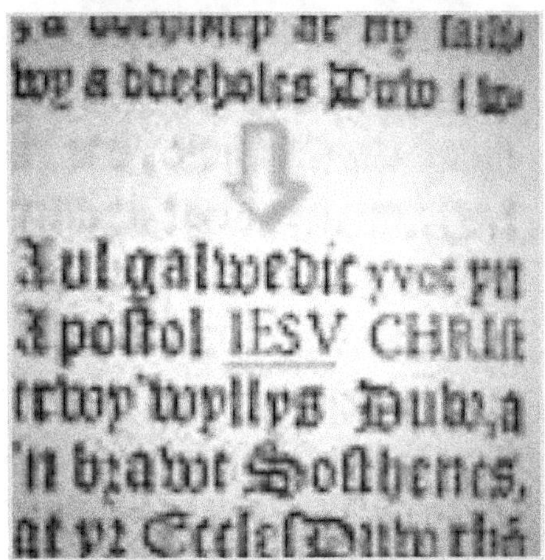

What Was The First Use Of The Word JESUS?

This word is well-known around the world, *yet it has no meaning in any language.* The letter J is less than 500 years old. The *SUS* component sounds like the Hebrew word for *horse*, <u>and</u> the Greek version of Nimrod, *ZEUS*.

The KJV used IESV in its first edition based on the Latin Vulgate it is translated from, but later began to use "JESUS" in later revisions.

Probably the first to use "JESUS" lived during the 16th century. It developed from the form ***IESV*** used since the 4th century. The greatest secret held by the secret societies started with the whisperers, and Inigo Loyola is a good candidate for being a promoter of the word JESUS.

In 1541 he founded a militant order called ***Societas IESV***, aka ***Society of JESUS***.

Excerpt from Wikipedia:

[quote]

Ignatius of Loyola, S.J., venerated as **Saint Ignatius of Loyola**, was a Spanish Catholic priest and theologian, who, with Peter Faber and Francis Xavier, founded the religious order of the *Society of Jesus* (The Jesuits), and became its first Superior General, in Paris in 1541. He envisioned the purpose of the Society of Jesus to be missionary work and teaching. In addition to the vows of chastity, obedience and poverty of other religious orders in the church, Loyola instituted a fourth vow for Jesuits of obedience to the Pope, to engage in projects ordained by the pontiff. Jesuits were instrumental in leading the Counter-Reformation.

As a former soldier, Ignatius paid particular attention to the spiritual formation of his recruits and recorded his method in the Spiritual Exercises (1548). In time, the method has become known as *"Ignatian spirituality."* [unquote]

Its another form of *spiritual captivity.*

Societas Iesu (Society of Jesus) was created to be a counter-reformation *militant order* of the Roman circus.

Regimini militantis Ecclesiae (Latin for *To the Government of the Church Militant)* was the title of the papal bull promulgated by Pope Paul III on September 27, 1540. This bull gave the first approval to the Society of Jesus, also known as the Jesuits, but at that time limited the number of

its members to sixty. The Jesuit Order's prime directive is to restore all worldly power to the papacy. The head was wounded when the nobility turned-away from accepting the pope as the head of the Roman Catholic Magisterium. *(Magisterium means teaching authority).*
Kings and nobles considered themselves to be Catholics, as the Anglican Catholic Circus of England remained steadfast to the traditions. The Jesuits plotted to use many barrels of gunpowder to blow-up King James and all of Parliament in 1605, but the plot was discovered at the last minute. (research *Gunpowder Plot*, 1605).

Adam Weishaupt S.J., was a Jesuit priest teaching theology in Bavaria until the Jesuit order was suppressed by the pope in 1773. The pope was poisoned, yet the suppression of the order remained for many years.
The Bavarian government also banned the order's activities. In 1776, Adam Weishaupt gave a new name to the society IESV; he called it the ILLUMINATI.
The nobility joined this elitist organization in large numbers, not knowing it was the renamed Jesuit order to continue its nefarious activities under a new disguise.
Adam Weishaupt once declared: *"Oh mortal man, is there nothing you can not be made to believe?"*

Adam Weishaupt designed the Great Seal
In Latin, the words declare an ominous message:
"Announcing the birth of a New World Order."
1776 is shown at the base of the pyramid in Roman Numerals. This is the year the Illuminati was formed.

THE HEBREW SCRIPT

The Hebrew Script as it may have appeared on the High Priest's

Golden Headpiece

Read from right-to-left, it reads: set-apart to Yahuah.
"QODESH L' YAHUAH"

YAHUAH'S NAME

Mishle / Proverbs 30:4: "*Who has gone up to the shamayim* [heavens] *and come down? Who has gathered the wind in His fists? Who has bound the mayim* [waters] *in a robe? Who established all the ends of the arets* [earth]*? What is His Name, and what is His Son's Name, if you know it?*

The answer is **Yahuah,** and **Yahusha; and He is ONE.**

Psalm 138:2:
"I bow myself toward Your qodesh Hekal, And give thanks to Your Name For Your kindness and for Your truth; For You have made great Your Word, Your Name, above all."

Is The Name Of Yahuah Important?
With that question in mind, consider Psalm 79:6-7:
"Pour out Your wrath on the nations that have not known You, and on reigns that have not called on Your Name, for they have devoured Yaqub and laid-waste his pasture."
How will they hear unless someone is sent to speak it?
In 2008 the pope issued a ***bull*** that the Name based on the *Tetragrammaton*, the four vowels in Hebrew, is ***forbidden*** to use in prayer, song, or worship. There is only one Name, and it's Hebrew (the language of Eber, Eberith).
**bull: a letter containing a direct order from the pope.*

YAHUSHA SPOKE EBERITH (HEBREW)

Acts 22:2 and 26:14 say that Shaul (later known as Paul) heard Yahusha *speaking to him in Eberith*, the language some translations have tried to alter by changing the word to *Aramaic*. The word "Aramaic" is _not_ found in any of the writings of the first Natsarim. The word *Aramaic* is inserted in some of the translations, which often contain *faulty interpretations*.

There was no letter "J" until the 16th century.
The Anglican Catholic Circus adopted **IESV** from the Latin Vulgate.
The KJV is the English translation of the Latin Vulgate.
The word JESUS was not placed in it until decades later.
Yahusha's only Name is Hebrew. (Acts 4:12)
He came in His Father's Name. It is expressed as the root word plus a suffix: YAHU + SHA, and becomes YAHUSHA. This Name means: ***"I am your Deliverer."***

James Strong published his concordance in 1890, and based his work on the **KJV**, an Anglican Catholic translation. James Strong was a Methodist theologian and professor.

1ˢᵗ Edition Authorized Version (KJV) showing IESV:

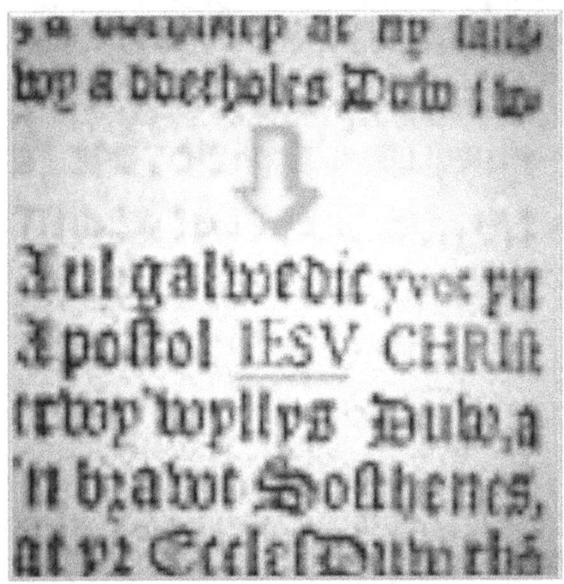

YAHUAH'S COMMANDS

Shemoth [Exodus] 20: *And Alahim spoke all these Words, saying,* [2] *"I am Yahuah your Alahim, who brought you out of* the *land of Mitsrayim* [Egypt], *out of the house of slavery.* [3] *You have no other mighty ones* [Gods and/or Lords] *against My face* [before Me] [4] *You do not make for yourself a carved image* [statue], *or any likeness* [paintings, statues or stained glass images] *of that which is in the shamayim* [heavens] *above, or which is in the arets* [earth] *beneath, or which is in the mayim* [waters] *under the arets,* [5] *you do not bow down to them nor serve them. For I, Yahuah your Alahim am a jealous Al, visiting the crookedness of the fathers on the children to the 3rd and 4th generations. Of those who hate Me,* [6] *but showing kindness to thousands, to those who love Me and guard* [keep] *My commands.* [7] *You do not cast the Name of Yahuah your Alahim to ruin.* [8] *Remember the Shabath day, to set it apart.* [9] *Six yomim* [days] *you labor, and shall do all your work,* [10] *but the 7th yom* [day] *(Saturday) is a Shabath of Yahuah your Alahim. You do not do any work – you, nor your son, nor your daughter, nor your male servant, nor your female servant, nor your cattle, nor your stranger who is within yours gates.* [11] *For in six yomim Yahuah made the shamayim and the arets, the sea and all that is in them, and rested the 7th yom. Therefore Yahuah blessed the Shabath day and set it apart.* [12] *Respect your father and your mother, so thar your yomim are prolonged upon the soil which Yahuah your Alahim is giving you.* [13] *You do not murder* [including yourselves and/or unborn children]. [14] *You do not break wedlock.* [15] *You do not steal.* [16] *You do not bear false witness against your neighbor.* [17] *You do not covet your neighbour's house, you do not covet your neighbour's ashah* [wife], *nor his male servant, nor his female servant, nor his ox, nor his donkey, or whatever belongs to your neighbor."* [18] *And all the people saw the thunders, and lightening flashes, the sound of the ram's horn, and the mountain smoking. And the people saw it, and they trembled and stood at a distance,* [19] *and said to Mosheh* [Moses], *"You speak with*

us and we hear, but let not Alahim speak with us, lest we die." [20]*And Mosheh said to the people "Do not fear, for Alahim has come to prove you, and in order that His fear be before you, so that you do not sin."*
...   In every place where I cause My Name to be remembered I shall come to you and bless you."

DISPENSATIONALISM:
aka REPLACEMENT THEOLOGY

Interpreting the Scriptures this way originated with **John Darby** in the nineteenth century, around 1830.
It began the idea that the adherents of Christianity **replaced** the tribes of Israel, and all the promises made to them were transferred to gentiles, *with no regard for obeying the Eternal Covenant.*

Meet John and Cyrus

Replacement Theology spread after the publication of the *Cyrus Scofield Reference Bible*, published in 1909.
YirmeYahu 31 stands in direct conflict with any idea that Yahuah will forget His people, *or His Covenant.*
Mt. 24:35: ***"The heaven and the arets shall pass away, but My Words shall by no means pass away."***
There is no way Yahuah will forsake His chosen people and replace them with lawless gentiles that disobey His Covenant and pretend they only have to believe. Read the

words He gave us about this at YirmeYahu / Jer. 31, and it will be apparent. Revelation 22:14-15 confirms there is a body of Commandments to be guarded, which are also brought up at Malaki 4:1-6. Ecclesiates 12:13-14 specifically tells us they are to be obeyed by all mankind.

Who has deceived us? The answer is, the teachers of tradition. Christianity is described perfectly in the book of Yekezqal / Ezekiel 22:25-27:

"There is a conspiracy of her prophets in her midst, like a roaring lion tearing the prey. They have devoured life, they have taken wealth and precious things, they have made many widows in her midst. Her priests have done violence to My teaching and they profane My qodesh things. They have not distinguished between the qodesh and profane, nor have they made known the difference between the unclean and the clean. And they have hidden their eyes from My Shabathuth, and I am profaned in their midst. Her leaders in her midst are like wolves tearing the prey, to shed blood, to destroy lives, and to get greedy gain."

The Decalogue Stone At Los Lunas, New Mexico

The Ten Commandments in original Hebrew are engraved on an ancient gatestone at Hidden Mountain. This unprotected stone is older than any other artifact connected to the descendants of the tribes of Yisharal, and it's located near Los Lunas, New Mexico, USA.

It was a colony founded during the days of Shalomoh (Solomon) around 900 BCE, and they wrote the Ten Commandments on their gate.

It was etched hundreds of years before the birth of YirmeYahu (Jer.), YashaYahu (Is.), Yekezqal (Ez.), Amus, Baruk, Danial, and many others.

A 3000-Year-Old Inscription On A Gate Stone At Los Lunas

Dt. / Debarim 6:4-9

"Hear, O Yisharal: Yahuah our Alahim, Yahuah is one! And you shall love Yahuah your Alahim with all your heart, and with all your being, and with all your might. And these Words which I am commanding you today shall be in your heart, and you shall impress them upon your children, and shall speak of them when you sit in your house, and when you walk by the way, and when you lie down, and when you rise up, and shall bind them as a sign on your hand, and they shall be as frontlets between your eyes. And you shall write them on the doorposts of your house and on your gates."

I AM YAHUAH ALAHIM-OF YOU WHO BROUGHT YOU OUT FROM LAND OF MITSRAYIM FROM HOUSE OF

SLAVERIES. NOT HE SHALL BE TO YOU ALAHIM OTHER ONES BEFORE FACE OF ME

NOT YOU MAKE FOR SELF IDOL OR ANY IMAGE THAT IN SKIES FROM ABOVE OR THAT

ON ARETS FROM BENEATH OR THAT IN WATERS FROM BENEATH TO ARETS NOT YOU BOW

TO THEM AND NOT YOU WORSHIP THEM FOR I AM YAHUAH AL OF YOU AL JEALOUS, PUNISHING

SIN OF FATHERS ON CHILDREN TO THIRDS AND TO FOURTH TO ONES HATING ME BUT SHOWING LOVE

O THOUSANDS TO ONES LOVING ME AND TO ONES GUARDING OF COMMANDS OF ME. NOT YOU TAKE NAME YAHUAH

ALAHIM OF YOU FOR RUIN FOR NOT HE HOLD GUILTLESS YAHUAH WHO TAKES NAME OF HIM

FOR RUIN. TO REMEMBER DAY OF THE SHABATH TO SEPARATE; SIX OF DAYS YOU SHALL LABOR

AND YOU SHALL DO ALL OF WORK OF YOU BUT DAY OF THE SEVENTH IS SHABATH TO YAHUAH ALAHIM OF YOU

NOT YOU DO ANY OF WORK YOU OR SON OF YOU OR DAUGHTER OF YOU MANSERVANT OF YOU

OR MAIDSERVANT OF YOU OR ANIMAL OF YOU OR ALIEN OF YOU WHO WITHIN GATES OF YOU

FOR SIX OF DAYS HE MADE YAHUAH THE SKIES AND THE ARETS

THE SEA AND ALL THAT IN THEM BUT HE RESTED ON THE DAY THE SEVENTH

FOR THIS HE BARUK YAHUAH DAY OF THE SHABATH AND HE MADE SEPARATE HIM

HONOR FATHER OF YOU AND MOTHER OF YOU THAT THEY MAY BE LONG DAYS OF YOU

IN THE LAND THAT YAHUAH ALAHIM OF YOU GIVING TO YOU

NOT YOU MURDER NOT YOU BREAK WEDLOCK NOT YOU STEAL

NOT YOU GIVE AGAINST NEIGHBOR OF YOU TESTIMONY OF FALSE

NOT YOU COVET HOUSE OF NEIGHBOR OF YOU NOT YOU COVET WIFE OF NEIGHBOR OF YOU

OR MANSERVANT OR MAIDSERVANT OR OX OR DONKEY OR ANYTHING OF YOUR NEIGHBOR

Love Commands

The Ten Commands (instructions) are the Truth we all need to see as instructions teaching us *how to love*. Doing them,

not just hearing them, results in Yahusha's help to keep us on the path. He gives His Spirit ONLY to those who *obey* Him. (Acts 5:32). To know Who love is becomes the great reward for those seeking Him. Those who speak to one another and honor the Name of Yahuah have been described as Yahuah's treasured possession, and their names are in a scroll of rememberance. We discern the difference between the upright and the lawless.
See Malaki 3

Wait until Revelation 22:14-15 is read and understood by the billions of people pastors have deceived.
The pastors tell them the Ten Commandments were annulled so they could tell us about dispensationalism, also known as *historical progression.* Instead of teaching us the Eternal Covenant of love, they control what is taught, and who teaches.

APOCRYPHA - *Obscurity Of Origin:*
Apocrypha are works, usually written, of unknown authorship or of doubtful origin.
The word apocryphal (ἀπόκρυφος) was first applied to writings which were kept *secret* because they were the vehicles of esoteric knowledge considered too profound or too sacred to be disclosed to anyone other than the *initiated.* Inspired writings build us up and *encourage obedience.* Outside writings produce *chaos and confusion.*
 "See to it that no one makes a prey of you through philosophy and empty deceit, which are based on

human tradition and the spiritual forces of the world rather than on Mashiak." Kolossians 2:8

WHAT IS SIN?
Sin is the transgression of the Turah (1 Yahukanon / Jn. 3:4). If one is guilty of intentionally breaking the eternal Covenant. there remains no more offering for sin (Eberim / Heb. 10:18).

STRANGE FIRE
We can't make stuff up and expect Yahusha to like it.
CELIBACY - What's That About?
This is one of many strange behaviors discussed among a stream of other traditions invented by the Magisterium (teaching authority). The reason for celibacy is revealed on my youtube channel, Lew White, then on my channel search for a video called **TIMELINE**.
It will show when each dogma developed in Catholicism from the year 300 to the present day. It will blow your mind.

Do not add nor take away from the instructions.
"He who turns his ear away from hearing Turah, even his prayer is an abomination." - Proverbs 28:9
Watch it and share it with those trapped by the philosophies of men.

Attacking The Unborn

Yahuah's vengeance will one day be unleashed. He said:
Exodus 21:22-25: ***"And when men strive and they shall smite a pregnant ashah** [wife]**, and her children come out, yet there is no injury, he shall certainly be punished accordingly as the ashah's husband lays upon him. And he shall give through the judges. But if there is injury, then you shall give life for life, eye for eye, tooth for tooth, hand for hand, foot for foot, burn for burn, wound for wound, lash for lash."***

IDOLATRY

Exodus 23:13: ***"And in all that I have said to you take heed. And make no mention of the name of other mighty ones*** [Lords, Gods, Jesus Christ, Holy Spirit, etc. etc.]***, let it not be heard from your mouth."***

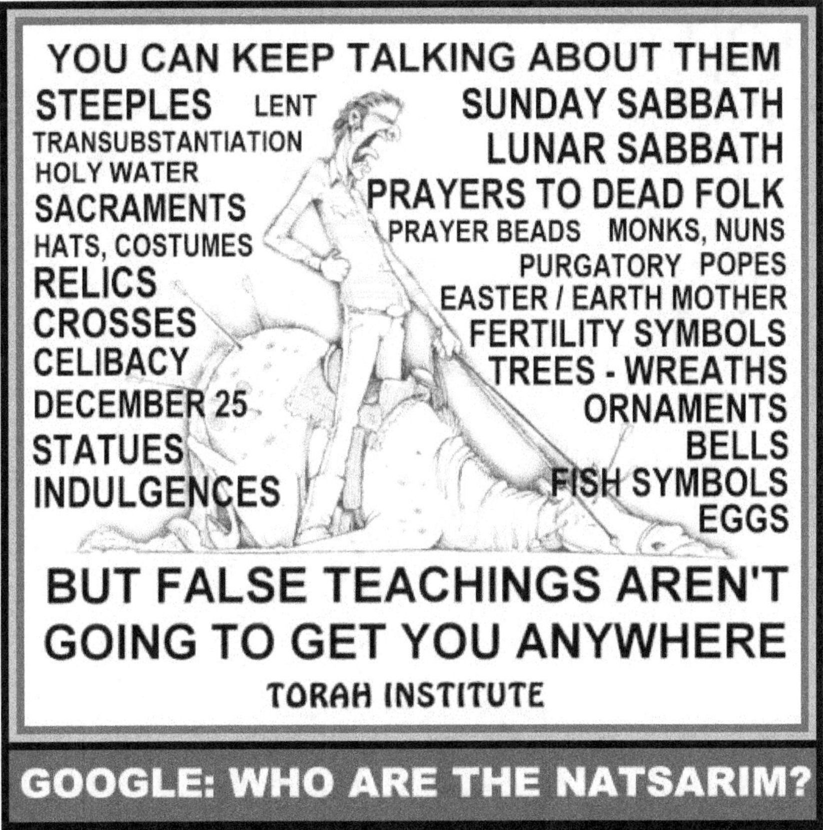

Yahuah's Name will overthrow all His enemies:

Exodus 23:20-25: ***"See, I am sending a Messenger before you to guard you in the way and to bring you to the place which I have prepared. Be on guard before Him and obey His voice. Do not rebel against Him, for He is not going to pardon your transgressions, for My Name is in Him. But if you diligently obey His voice and shall do all that I speak, then I shall be an enemy to your enemies and a distresser to those who distress you. For My Messenger shall go before you and shall bring you to the Amorites and the Kittites and the Perizzites and the Kenanites and the Kuis and the Yebusis, and I shall cut them off. Do not bow down to their mighty ones, nor serve them, nor do according to their works, but without fail overthrow them and without fail break down their pillars. And you shall serve Yahuah your Alahim, and He shall bless your bread and your water. And I shall remove sickness from your midst."***

A warning to the Korinthians

I Korinthians 6:9-10:
"Do you not know that the unrighteous shall not inherit the reign of Yahuah? Do not be deceived. Neither those who whore, nor idolaters, nor adulterers, nor effeminate, nor homosexuals [arseno-kolital: *arsen, male; koiltos, intercourse*], ***nor thieves, nor greedy of gain, nor drunkards, nor revilers, nor swindlers shall inherit the reign of Yahuah."***

Revelation 22:14-15:
"Blessed are those doing His commands so that the authority shall be theirs to the tree of life, and to enter through the gates into the city. But outside are the dogs and those who enchant with drugs, and those who whore, and the murderers, and the idolaters, and all those who love and do falsehood."

The World Is *Completely* Deceived

The one Name of our Deliverer (Acts 4:12) is YAHUSHA.
Revelation 22:14-15 (quoted above) is enough to terrify those deceived by Christian pastors.
If we remove their masks, we will see they do not know YAHUSHA.
This is confirmed by 1 Jn. / Yahukanon 2:4.

WHAT WAS THE OLD COVENANT?

The **old covenant** was written on a **scroll** and placed beside the Ark (Dt. 31:26). It prescribed animal blood for temporary atonement for accidental transgressions.

The renewal of the covenant in Yahusha's blood made the old covenant OBSOLETE, and He accomplished our complete and *permanent redemption* (Eberim 8:13). Yahusha could not obey all 613 details the Talmud cites; He is a male, so the instructions for females do not apply to males. Also, the entire old covenant with animal offerings for transgressions have grown old and have become **obsolete** by His ONE offering of Himself. ***The Ruach ha Qodesh purchased us with His Own blood - and His Name is Yahusha.***

What is His Name, and what is His Son's Name?

In the case of the inspired Word of Yahuah, there has been a long-standing resistance to uttering the Name.

In the 8th century, a sophisticated method using vowel marks was developed, and it has been promoted successfully for many centuries and is the official delusion now. It has been the primary lock keeping everyone from calling on the Name.

We have the Key, and we're the guardians of the Name.

We are the Natsarim, the first followers of Yahusha.

Here in the last days, Yahusha is awakening His bride, those having stored up the extra oil of His Name. The conspiracy to conceal His Name is being shouted from the rooftops.

This is the apostasy (***falling-away***) that must come first. (**2 Thess. 2:3**)

Are you feeling the urges from Yahusha to **come out** from men's teachings?

One of the problems of getting to the Truth has always been a **teaching authority** stepping in to make it seem the "lay person" doesn't have the capacity, training, or permission granted to them to teach. This was how they treated Yahusha, because He released so much Truth He became a threat to the fragile egos of those controlling teachings. Yahusha is our Teacher, not traditions invented by men. The Name is the Key of knowledge, the Rock rejected by the builders. (**Ps. 118:26**)

Because He Has Known My Name (Ps. 91:14)

How does it matter that we know the Name of Yahusha, and search-out how it became concealed? Proverbs 30:4 asks,

"What is His Name, and what is His Son's Name, if you know it?" The identity of Yahusha is only revealed to those He chooses to reveal it (Mt. 11:27). He is Yahuah, but was not recognized at the time He visited us in the body He prepared for Himself to indwell. He purchased us with His own blood (Acts 20:28).

The Sanhedrin forbade the use of His Name 2000 years ago, and a papal bull in 2008 did the same. YashaYahu 42:8 is very specific, and the importance of knowing the identity of the Creator by His Name is clear at YirmeYahu 10:25, Psalm 79:6, 91:14, Revelation 1, Shemoth 3:14-15, 6:3, Malaki 3:16, and dozens of other texts. The most-used word in the inspired text is the four-vowels, **yod-hay-uau-hay**.

The dragon has worked diligently to suppress the Name of Yahuah by directing his servants to omit it from popular translations (see any preface). Revelation 3:8 speaks to those who keep His Word, and have not denied His Name. If the Name doesn't matter, what's up with all these efforts He makes to say it does matter?

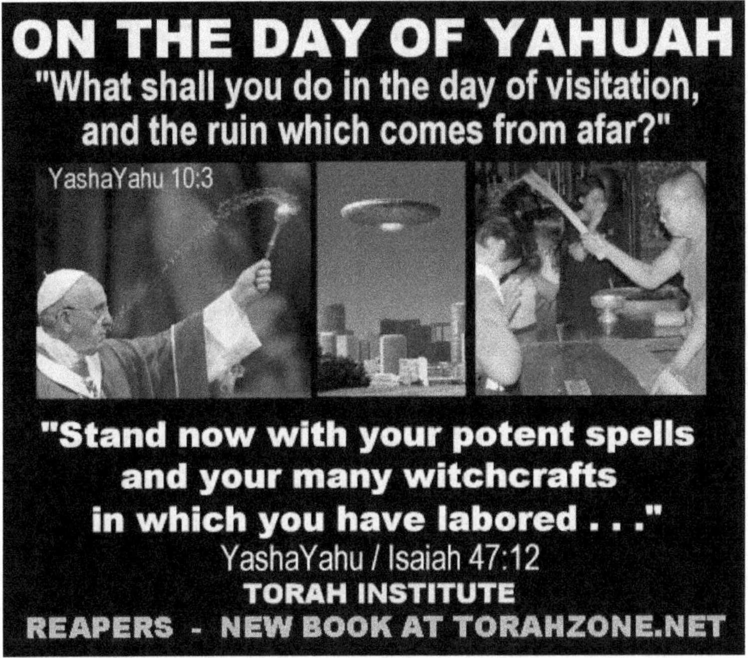

Sect of the NATSARIM
This is what Yahusha called His first followers (Yn. 15:5), and He is awakening His *last Natsarim* on the Earth in these last days. NATSARIM are referred to in the writings of the circus fathers (Alexandrian Culture), and today

as NOTSRIM by the Yahudim, and NASRANI by Muslims.
We have also been called Pasagians and Waldensians (pass
or valley-dwellers), hiding from the brutality of the
Magisterium, which persecuted us for guarding the
Everlasting Covenant, and rejecting their ecclesiastical
authority.
ACTS 24:5 shows that Paul was accursed of being
"a ringleader of the sect of the Natsarim."

Danial 12 describes an awakening in the distress of the last
days. Yahusha mentioned this distress to His Natsarim, telling us to
     pray our flight not be in winter, or on a yom Shabath.
(See Mt. 24:20)

Yahusha is turning the world upside down again (as at Acts
17), and *many are now calling on His Name to be delivered.*

Yahusha is about to send His harvesters to remove the weeds
and burn them, and gather us to meet Him at the marriage
supper of the Lamb.
Read Revelation 22 to see what has been restrained by
Christian pastors.

PAGANISM NORMALIZED
Pagan behavior has become accepted as normal.
It's easy to fool someone, but difficult to convince them they
have been fooled. Yahusha is the Living Word.
His penetrating gaze can see what is behind the thoughts and
intentions of everyone.
Above all else, a worldly person seeks to possess *pleasure,
possessions, and power.* Because they want their way in all
things, they want Yahuah to give them whatever they ask of
Him. This thinking pattern is reinforced by the false shepherds
they have heaped-up for themselves in great numbers.
These only say what their itching ears desire to hear.

WHAT SHALL I DO TO INHERIT ETERNAL LIFE?
Yahusha brought our attention to how hard it is to apprehend
the reign of Yahuah due to the motives common to us all who
have not come to know Him:
*"And a certain ruler asked Him, saying, 'Good Teacher, **what***

shall I do to inherit everlasting life?'
Yahusha said to him, 'Why do you call Me good? No one is
good except One – **Alahim**.
You know the Commands, Do not break wedlock,
Do not murder, Do not steal, Do not bear false witness,
Respect your father and your mother.'
And he said, 'All these I have guarded from my youth.'
And hearing this, Yahusha said to him, 'Yet one you lack:
Sell all that you have and distribute to the poor, and you shall
have treasure in heaven. And come, follow Me.'
But when he heard this, he became intensely sad because he was
extremely rich. And when Yahusha saw that he became intensely
sad, He said,
'How hard it is for those who have riches to enter into the
reign of Yahuah! For it is easier for a camel to enter through a
needle's eye* than for a rich man to enter into the reign of
Yahuah.' And those who heard it said, 'And who is able to be
delivered?" Luke 18:18-26 BYNV
***Needle's eye:** a small hole, see Ezek 12
Under siege, the **rich carry no more** through the wall to
escape **than the poor.** The point here is to leave all your
wealth behind and **escape with your life.**

The answer to the question, "Who is *able* to be delivered?"
No one Is able without Yahuah. *Note the word,* **<u>with</u>**:
**"And He said, 'What is impossible with men is possible
<u>with</u> Alahim.'"** Luke 18:27 BYNV

Do Angels Worship Yahusha?
Philippians 2:5-11:
*"For, let this mind be in you which was also in Mashiak
Yahusha, Who, being the essence of Yahuah, considered it
not theft to be the same as Yahuah; yet emptied Himself,
taking the form of a servant, and came to be in the likeness of
men. And having been perceived in the form of a man, He
humbled Himself and became obedient to death, death even
of a stake. Yahuah, therefore, has highly exalted Him and
given Him the Name which is above every name, that at the
Name of Yahusha every knee should bow, of those in heaven,
and of those on arets, and of those under the arets, and every
tongue should admit that Yahuah is Yahusha Mashiak, to the
esteem of Yahuah the Father."*

Kolossians 2:8-10:
See to it that no one makes a prey of you through philosophy and empty deceit, according to the tradition of men, according to the elementary things of the world, and not according to Mashiak. Because in Him dwells all the Fullness of Yahuah bodily, and you have been made complete in Him, Who is the Head of all principality and authority."

1 Korinthians 12:3:
"Therefore I make known to you that no one speaking by the Ruach of Yahuah says Yahusha is a curse, and no one is able to say that Yahusha is Aduni except by the Ruach ha Qodesh."

Hebrews - Eberim 1:1-6:
Yahuah, having of old spoken in many portions and many ways to the fathers by the prophets, has in these last Yomim spoken to us by the Son, whom He has appointed heir of all, through whom also He made the ages, Who being the brightness of the esteem and the exact representation of His substance, and sustaining all by the Word of His power, having made a cleansing of our sins through Himself, sat down at the right hand of the Greatness on high,
having become so much better than the messengers, as He has inherited a more excellent Name than them. For to which of the messengers did He ever say, "You are My Son, today I have brought You forth"? And again, "I shall be to Him a Father, and He shall be to Me a Son"?
And when He again brings the firstborn into the world, He says,
"Let all the messengers of Yahuah do reverence to Him."

YashaYahu 43:10-15:
*"You are My witnesses," says Yahuah, "And My servant whom I have chosen, so that you know and believe Me, and understand that I am He. Before Me there was no Al formed, nor after Me there is none. "I, I am Yahuah, and besides Me there is no deliverer. I, I have declared and delivered, and made known, and there was no foreign mighty one among you. And you are My witnesses," says Yahuah, "**that I am Al.** Even from the yom I am He, and no one delivers out of My hand. I work, and who turns it back?" Thus said*

Yahuah, your Redeemer, the Qodesh One of Yisharal, "For your sake I shall send to Babel, and bring them all down as fugitives, even the Kaldeans, who rejoice in their ships. I am Yahuah, your Qodesh One, Creator of Yisharal, your King."

Yes, angels bow and worship Yahusha.
We are His **ambassadors** (2 Korinthians 5:20).
He is Alahim, and we are His witnesses.

The 1945 Encyclopedia Americana has this to say under to topic GOD:
"GOD (god) Common Teutonic word for personal object of religious worship, formerly applicable to super-human beings of heathen myth; on conversion of Teutonic races to Christianity, term was applied to Supreme Being."

Proverbs 28:9 is alarming when it is properly understood. Praying to Yahuah while remaining disobedient?
He says it's an abomination.

WHO IS YAHUSHA?
YAHUSHA [H3091] is YAHUAH [H3068]
Prepare to meet Him, *He's at the door.*
Yahusha is the Name to call on for deliverance, meaning "I am your Deliverer." The word YAHUSHA is a transliteration of yod-hay-uau-shin-ayin.
Yahusha said He is Al Shaddai (Rev. 1:8), the same Alahim Who spoke to Mushah to tell Farah to let His people go (Shemoth / Exodus 6:3).
Yahuah is one, and there is no other deliverer before or after Him (YashaYahu 43:11).
Every knee will bow to the Name Yahusha when He returns to take His eternal reign (Philippians 2:10-11). If we know Yahusha, we know the Father also (Yahukanon / John 8:19, 14:7, Proverbs 30:4).
Everyone should Google the Name YAHUSHA.
It is the Name that will turn the world upside-down (What happened at Acts 17 is happening - again!).
Watch "I AM HE" - https://youtu.be/nYmv8rwJfes
A challenging video concerning Who Yahusha really is.

At Mt. 11:27 Yahusha said,
"no one knows the Son except the Father.

Nor does anyone know the Father except the Son, and he to whom the Son wishes to reveal Him."

Yahusha prepared to bring His message to us by fasting for 40 days and nights, and was then tempted by the devil.
Here is one of the interesting statements that emerges from that debate: (Mt. 4:5-7):
"Then the devil took Him up into the qodesh city, set Him on the edge of the Qodesh Place, and said to Him,
"If You are the Son of Alahim, throw Yourself down.
For it has been written,
'He shall command His messengers concerning you,' and,
'In their hands they shall bear you up, so that you do not dash your foot against a stone.'"
Yahusha said to him, "It has also been written,
'You shall not try Yahuah your Alahim.'"
Yahusha was quoting the Turah from Dt. 6:16.
He was telling the devil Who He really is.

Do you realize Who we are dealing with? If He is pursuing you, stop running away. Surrender now while He is near.

REDEEMED BY THE BLOOD OF THE LAMB
We are all dead until we receive the Life of Yahusha's Ruach, enabling us to believe He gave Himself for us, and in turn we give Him our vessels to be *His habitation* to walk in a newness of life. Our purpose becomes His purpose for us, and those arounds us ponder the change in our behavior.

They wonder why we no longer run with them to do the things we used to do:
"Therefore, since Mashiak suffered in the flesh, arm yourselves also with the same mind, because he who has suffered in the flesh has ceased from sin, so that he no longer lives the rest of his time in the flesh for the lusts of men, but according to the desire of Alahim. *For we have spent enough of our past lifetime in doing the desire of the nations, having walked in indecencies, lusts, drunkenness, orgies, wild parties, and abominable idolatries, in which they are surprised that you do not run with them in the same flood of loose behavior, blaspheming, who shall give an account to Him who is ready to judge the living and the dead. For this*

reason the besorah was also brought to those who are dead, so that, whereas they are judged according to men in the flesh, they might live according to Alahim in the Ruach."
1Peter 4:1-6

Be Careful How You Hear

It's vital to believe the Scriptures are inspired.
The question is, how much of the inspired Hebrew has been interpreted incorrectly by translators?
Many people are waking-up to the false traditions, and they are are also shocked to learn they've been using false names.
Uninspired words include: Easter, Bible, Jesus, LORD, and GOD.
Followers of Yahusha (Natsarim) obey Him, and He guides them.
The disobedience to the Eternal Covenant (Ten Commandments) is going to bring about the burning wrath of Yahuah, and He tells us why at Isaiah / YashaYahu 24:5.
To test what you hear, read: 1 Jn. 2:4 and Rev. 22:14-15.
Few teachers *obey* His Commandments, revealing they are liars.
The *restoration to favor* demands repentance and obedience; these are the evidence of our belief, through the indwelling Mind of Yahusha.

PEOPLE DON'T KNOW WHAT THEY DON'T KNOW

The difference between a *translation* and a *transliteration* is important for us to distinguish. The writers of Scripture used the Eberith language (today called Hebrew). The original Eberith is the only *inspired* text.

All the *translations* of Scripture into other languages are interpretations. The names of people and places can be *transliterated* to sound like the inspired words, but in most cases men's fingerprints have molested their phonology (sound). A *translation* interprets, but a *transliteration* attempts to make the exact sound of an inspired word, but uses a foreign alphabet to do so.

Shall we go on sinning so His favor may increase, pushing and testing the limits of His patience? Absolutely not!
The objective is not to adopt or hide the original pagan behavior thinking Yahuah will never remember what it is if we flip it into worshipping Him. He knows what it is, even if we don't know.
Steeples and obelisks are very ancient pagan pillars, and He hates them (see Lev. 26). How about all the obelisks, like we often see in graveyards all over the world?

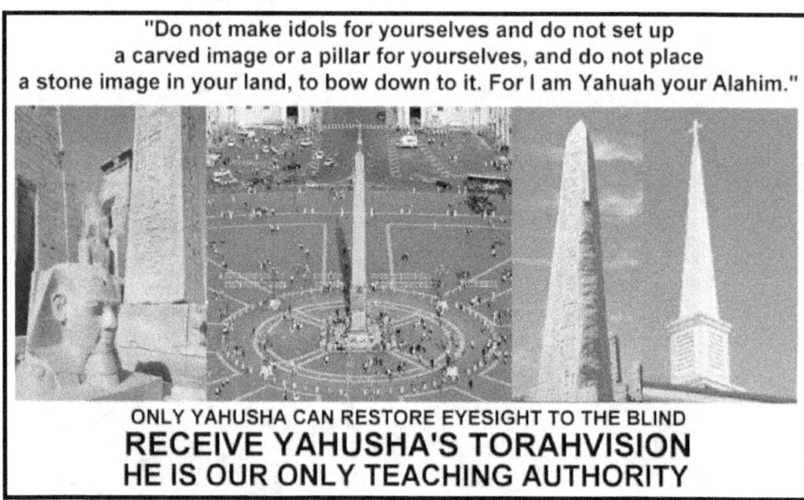

Where Is The Obelisk Of Caligula? *Vaticanus Mons!*

The obelisk is located in what is called Vatican City, squarely placed in front of the Cathedral of St. Peter.
Inside is the ancient Roman haloed statue of Jupiter they renamed "Peter," and its toes are worn smooth from all the

millions of visitors that have kissed them.

Vaticanus is an ancient Etruscan word, and was their name for a swampy hill used as a burial ground.

In the early 1st century, Caligula drained it and held orgiastic carnivals there. He built a racecourse at the site, into which he moved an *Egyptian obelisk from Heliopolis*.

(Heliopolis means "city of the Sun").

The obelisk standing in front of St. Peter's Cathedral is the same obelisk Caligula imported and placed in his racecourse at Vaticanus Mons. It is renowned as one of the seven hills of Rome (Vaticanus Mons / Hill).

The Romans used the name for a deity believed to endow speech to infants, as the first syllable is pronounced "UA," which they associated with the cry of a newborn child. The hill became known as Vaticum in Latin, and there is still a **Circus** (RCC) based at the site. It is riddled with underground tunnels, and human remains form the walls in some places (catacombs). If there was ever a search for the most appropriate site for the throne of satan, there are few places on this Earth that can match the history of debauchery and defilement this hill can claim among its qualifications.

DO YOU WANT TO FIND YAHUAH?

Yahuah said **if we seek Him** with all our heart, we will find Him. Yahuah exists, and the meaning of His Name communicates a transcendence of all time as we perceive it. He is everywhere in all time and space, an ever-present Being without beginning or ending, and Whose Name could be interpreted from Rev. 1:8 to mean:

I *WAS* RIGHT HERE
I *AM* RIGHT HERE
I *WILL BE* RIGHT HERE

Those who believe He exists and diligently seek Him will find Him. *"But without belief it is impossible to please Him, for he who comes to Yahuah has to believe that He is, and that He is a rewarder of those who earnestly seek Him."* Hebrews 11:6
What is impossible for men is possible with Yahuah. Knowing His Word transforms the mind of the flesh into His pattern of thought, taking on the perspective of His Spirit.
"Not by might, nor by power, but by My Ruach, says Yahuah

Yahuah Is One
Yaqub 2:17-22:
*"Show me your belief without your works, and I shall show you
my belief **by my works**. You believe that Alahim is one. You
do well. The demons also believe – and shudder! But do
you wish to know, O foolish man, that the belief without the
works is dead? Was not Abrahim our father declared right
by works when he offered Yitshaq his son on the altar?
Do you see that the belief was working with his works, and by
the works the belief was perfected?"*

Our **obedience** changes everything. When we obey the eternal
Covenant, we perfect and confirm our belief. We then receive the
help of Yahusha indwelling us, but until we obey, He will not give us
His Ruach (Acts 5:32).

YOU HAVE TO QUESTION TEACHINGS
"Come, you children, listen to me; Let me teach you the fear
of Yahuah. Who is the man who desires life, who loves many
days, in order to see good? Keep your tongue from evil, and
your lips from speaking deceit. Turn away from evil and do
good; seek peace, and pursue it. The eyes of Yahuah are on
the **righteous***, and His ears unto their cry." Psalm 34:11-15
*obedient ones

TRANSFORMATION OF PAGANISM
Truth has fallen in the streets, and trampled by teachers!
Acts 18 mentions the early expulsions of Torah-guarding
Yahudim from the city of Rome by emperor Claudius a few
years prior to the destruction of Yerushalem.
The 2nd century elder **Polycarp of Smyrna wrote** a letter to
Victor, a fellow elder in Rome, discouraging the observance of
The pagan **Easter***, and encourages **Passover**.
*uninspired word at Acts 12:3 (aka Eostre, Ishtar, Astoroth)
Polycrates emphatically stated that he was following the
patterns passed down to him:
"We observe the exact day; neither adding, nor taking away.
For in Asia also great lights have fallen asleep, which shall
rise again on the day of the Master's coming ... All these
observed the 14th day for the Passover according to the

besorah, deviating in no respect, but following the rule of belief. And I also, Polycrates, the least of you all, do according to the patterns of my relatives, some of whom I have closely followed. For seven of my relatives were elders; and I am the eighth. And my relatives always observed the day when the people ***put away the leaven***."

Emperor Theodosius (378-398) enforced Constantine's Catholicism to be the State Religion of the Roman Empire, and made church **membership compulsory**.
The forced-converts filled the assemblies with unregenerate pagans, and the state continued to tax those who observed other beliefs. At the websites below you may download a free tract / article with more details on how the Roman **Fiscus Judaicus** (Roman tax on Torah observers) slowly transformed the behavior of all the assemblies planted by the first Natsarim into steeple-building pagans, observing Sun-day and eating swine. They do not even know the real Name of their Redeemer, but have accepted another name, the name of an imposter. They do not live anything like Yahusha lived, which the following text insists we do:
"But if anyone guards His Word, the love of Alahim has truly been perfected in him. By this we know we are in Him; whoever claims to know Him must walk as Yahusha walked."
1 Yn. 2:5-6

Fundamental misunderstandings are being over-thrown in these last days as we see them described at Danial 12:1-13.

The Old Covenant: A Scroll, Or Tablets?

Dt. 31:26 says,
"Take this book (SEFER) *of the Law* (TORAH, instruction) *and place it __beside__ the ark of the Covenant of Yahuah your Alahim, that it may be there as a witness against you."*
The instructions written on the SEFER (scroll) were the priests' procedures to slaughter animals and temporarily cover the **unintentional sins** of the nation with the **imperfect blood of animals**.
That's the **TORAH** that has passed-away, having grown "old" and obsolete, and it is described at Hebrews chapters 8 –11. It's the old priesthood, now replaced with the renewed priesthood of Melkizedek and **Yahusha's perfect blood**.

The TORAH written on the stone tablets was not placed **beside** the ark, but safe, and **treasured**, inside. It is now written on the hearts of all those who have received a love for the Truth, circumcised inwardly by Yahusha Mashiak.
Do you see how the lie has deceived us?
The Ten Commandments are the eternal Covenant, and It **teaches us how to love.**

WE MUST STOP BEING IDOLATORS

The date and all the symbols used for ***Christmas*** is inherited from heathen worship and their customs.
The modern Santa Claus figure is masking the identity of Nimrod, a dreadful king known as all the solar deities born on December 25th in every time and place. Molok is one of his names, and children were incinerated in the lap / belly of the image of this Moabite idol. Our pastors have passed-down only lies and futility - ***go ask them why.***
Yahusha is right here, right now!

Paganism is all around us right now also.

MITHRAS
APOLLO
LIBERTAS

OPEN YOUR EYES
SHIVA TEMPLES
FOSSILIZEDCUSTOMS.COM
YAHUSHA
RUSSIAN ORTHODOX
MOSQUES
IS COMING
THE WHORE SITS ON THE WATERS - REVELATION 17
US CAPITOL
SHIVA TEMPLE
SHIVA SHRINE
TEMPLE OF SHIVA & SHAKTI
ROMAN BASILICA
ON YAHUAH'S TEMPLE MOUNT
HINDU SHIVA SHRINE
ROME
OPENLY SERVING THE DESTROYER

The exoteric (external – as understood by the outsiders, masses) meaning of the Christmas tree is not understood as the fertility symbol it is ***esoterically*** known to be (internally understood by those initiated in the *secret mysteries* of witchcraft).

The ***ball-drop*** at the arrival of New Years' Day is another occult practice, and also refers to Nimrod.

A male's testicles drop around the time of their birth. In Ireland and other places, the new year witchcraft ceremonies involve *two* balls. Many people are decorating with one huge red ornament these days, which esoterically refers to the Sun, and Nimrod is the first to be worshipped as a solar deity.

All other solar deities are Nimrod, only the name is babbled by the other cultures. All share December 25th as their birthday.

The Nimrod culture is a retrograde force.

It's odd how people don't recognize the common origin of many objects and customs, and kill one another over them. The Islamic immigrants are violently opposed to the cultural background of the nations they find themselves in, and one element they find very distasteful is the "christmas tree."

This object is an ancient esoteric device embraced by Christianity, yet it represents the same thing as the domes on their mosques, including the famous "Dome of the Rock."

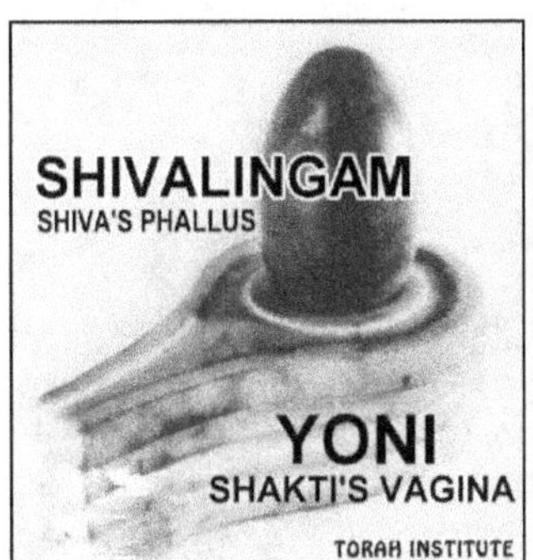

These are esoteric images of male fertility, only properly understood by those who are initiated in their occult consortiums. Their exoteric meanings are only for the masses. The upright tree, round ornaments, and tinsel have esoteric symbolism just as the domes on shrines and buildings associated with *ruling the masses (Nicolaitanes)*,

They are images of the *destroyer*, Shiva.

Islam was designed by the Vatican as a mechanism for the papacy to move to Yerushalayim.

It's focus is on **jihad** (war, struggle), and is a reflection of the Roman Catholic Magisterium's *Regimini Militante Ecclesiae.*

It is a tyrannical political, governmental, judicial, and economic authority *posing* as a religious institution. It's a masquerade.

Just like mother Babel, its behavior shows that it seeks to control the world.

ROSARIES - NECROMANCY

The prayer beads which monks and nuns wear, and are sold to the **laity** [commoners] in Catholicism, came into their system around CE 1090, about the same time *indulgences* and *celibacy* were embraced. Prayer beads originated with pagans, and are very common among Buddhists and Muslims. The Rudraksha beads of the Buddhists have 108 beads, and are sometimes *seeds*. The Muslims use 99 sacred stones on their rosaries, and Catholics have 59. During the time that the lands of Spain and Portugal were controlled by the Islamic Moors, a city was established called *Fatima*, named after one of Muhammad's daughters.

Mat 6:7 "And when praying, do not keep on babbling like the gentiles. For they think that they shall be heard for their many words."

The story is that three Catholic children met an apparition of "Mary" in Fatima, and the apparition gave one of them the prayer beads to pray to her with. Mary worship had started in CE 431, and grew more and more over the centuries. Mary is in the news quite often still, popping up in people's houses, on burned toast, or in the clouds. Catholics rally to see her. It is an odd thing, but Muslims also pray to Mary, because Muhammad married a Roman Catholic nun named Kadijah, and learned to venerate Mary from her. They only pray to Allah and Mary, yet they don't pray to Muhammad. Both Muhammad and Mary are dead people, rotting in the ground. In the US, a state is named for Mary: **Maryland**. Pagans' *repetitive prayers* are condemned by Yahusha.
Notice Mt. 6:7:
"And when you pray, do not keep on babbling like pagans, for they think they will be heard because of their many words. Do not be like them, for your Father knows what you need before you ask Him." Also, Dt. 18 and YashaYahu (Is.) 8 forbid prayer to any entity other than Yahuah. Contacting the dead is absolutely forbidden. Intercessory prayer may be done by living saints for other saints, but prayers **TO** the dead are an abomination.
Any contact with spirits is a grievous transgression known as

divination, and it is demonic.

PARTING OF WAYS; HOW ONE BECAME TWO
Tax Pressure Caused A Schism After The Second Temple Period

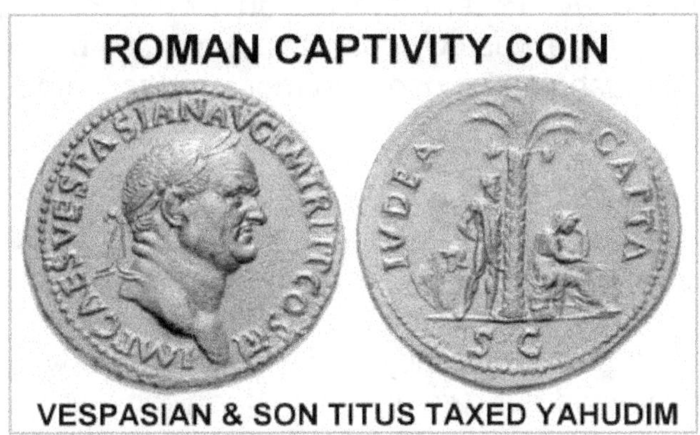

A TAX CALLED THE FISCUS IUDAICUS
The *fiscus Iudaicus* (Latin for "Jewish tax") or *fiscus Judaicus* was a tax-collecting directive instituted to collect the tax imposed by emperor Vespasian on Yahudim (Ioudaios/Jews) over all the Roman Empire after the destruction of Yerushalaim and its Temple in 70 CE. Revenues were directed to support the temple of Jupiter Optimus Maximus in Rome.

Persons who *behaved* like the Yahudim, or met with them to study Torah-observance, whether or not they were believers in Yahusha, were taxed. This tax usurped the tithe that was originally sent to support the Temple. It was redirected to lavishly support the pagan Roman religious institutions.

The only way to be exempt: abandon Yahudaism.

YAHUDAISM TO CHRISTIANITY
Before the Temple was destroyed in 70 CE, there was **no separation** whatsoever between those who believed Yahusha is the Mashiak from those who did not.

Luke's 2nd writing, Acts, is a record spanning about 30 to 32 years. It was written between 60-62 CE, during the horrific reign of Nero. The emperor Claudius had expelled all Yahudim from Rome in 49 CE, and we know Aquila and Priscilla were of those expelled. Paul met with them at Korinth. Acts 18:2:

"And he found a certain Yahudi named Aquila, born in Pontos, who had recently come from Italy with his wife

*__Priscilla, because Claudius had commanded all the
Yahudim to leave Rome – and he came to them."__*
About 3 years before Paul wrote the letter to the Romans,
Nero lifted the edict of Claudius, so Yahudim were permitted
to live at Rome again. Even in the late 50's when Paul wrote
to the Romans, there was no separation or parting between
believers in Yahusha and those who met together without
believing.

Luke recorded Acts only those few years prior to the
destruction of Yerushalayim. After the year 70, the pressure of
taxation on anyone that observed Torah became a factor in
developing new behavioral patterns and terminology.
Because the Roman tax agency was watching closely, gentile
converts felt they did not owe the fiscus Iudaiscus, so they
slowly withdrew and met separately. To appear distinguished,
they made as many changes as possible.
Sun worship changed its clothing.

TAX PRESSURE CAUSED CHANGES
 Even before the destruction of Yerushalayim, Rome was watching
those who would not worship their emperors and pay homage to their
deities. For this, the Yahudim already had their attention.
To the Romans, those who believed in Yahusha were a part of the
same body of people because they observed Torah in exactly the
same way, and met with one another. There are three perspectives;
that of the pagan Roman magisterium, the Yahudim who observed
Torah and the traditions of the fathers, and the new third group
among them, the Natsarim. The Natsarim consisted of both former
gentiles as well as those of the natural branches of Yisharal.
Because of the **fiscus Iudaicus**, those of the formerly gentile faction
contemplated how they were different, and should be treated as
distinct by those imposing the tax. This distinction didn't matter at all,
since they behaved exactly the same even if they did meet
separately from the main congregation they had once been a part of.
We see this even today, as congregations split apart for one reason
or another. With the aggravation of taxation, and being aware *the
tribute was used to support the pagan magisterium,* a gradual shift
began to take place as more converts entered the fold.
The average pagan Roman citizen was living in a world that
worshipped Mithras. Their meetings took place in caverns or rooms
built to resemble caverns, with an indoor altar at one end of the

space. The initiates progressed through grades or levels, similar to the method seen today in Masonry. More Mithraic mysteries were revealed as the adherent progressed to higher grades. A "**mystagogue**" explained the mysteries and theology to the initiate.

Very early, unconverted pagans became joined to the body of true believers, just as we see in groups today. As more converts from the pagan world entered into the congregations of those motivated to avoid paying the fiscus Iudaiscus, the more the behavior and surroundings took on their manner. Aspects such as steeples, icons, genuflecting, holy water, indoor altars, haloes, or statues were never part of the culture of Yisharal. To a Roman taxing official, the appearance of the "new Christian" assembly would have been mostly like the Mithras worshippers. The worshippers of Serapis at Alexandria were called "Christians," so adopting this label helped shield the now-corrupted followers of Yahusha from appearing to be "Jewish". Adopting all the accessories and gimmickry of the pagans, the new group could attract far greater numbers from the general population. The ignorant masses of pagans used the symbol of the crux widely as a symbol for the sun, and so by the time of Constantine it became adopted to link christ with Apollo, Constantine's most favored deity. As the dirty snowball grew larger, the Latin language translation by Eusebius Sophronius Hieronymus (Jerome) brought the term **crux** into the text, avoiding the word **stauro**, the Latin equivalent to the Greek **stauros**. Now, the new faith even had a logo, the former symbol of Sun worship: the **solar cross**.

Lawrence Schiffman (Yeshiva University) writes: *"The split between Judaism and Christianity did not come about simply or quickly. . . Further, the question of legal status as seen through Roman eyes also had some relationship to the issue."*

"The Romans at first regarded the Christians as part of the Jewish people. When Christianity spread and took on a clearly different identity, as acknowledged by both Jews and Christians, the Roman government modified its view. The emperor Nerva (96–98 C.E.) freed the Christians (probably including the Jewish Christians) from paying the fiscus judaicus, the Jewish capitation tax decreed as a punishment in the aftermath of the revolt of 66–73 C.E. Clearly, the Romans now regarded the Christians as a separate group. The way was paved for the legitimization of Christianity as a licit religion. The decline of the old pagan cults, coupled with the tremendous success

of Christianity, would eventually lead to the acceptance of the new faith as the official religion of the Roman Empire in 324 C.E." Lawrence H. Schiffman, *From Text to Tradition, Ktav Publishing House*, Hoboken, NJ, 1991.

Because the taxing authorities were constantly snooping around, it was advantageous to appear and sound completely distinct in every way. *Trying to appear different, the Hebrew roots were masked as much as possible*, so **changing terms** and **altering names** became acceptable.

Paganism became normalized.

The Greek texts eliminated the Name, and put in its place a **code**, in case a snooping tax agent were to examine them.

In place of the Name Yahusha, a secretive *Christogram* was used, which could only be understood through a mystagogue. The "IY" (IU) in Greek manuscripts is an *encoded Christogram*, usually with a **bar** over the letters (a **titlos**, meaning title), a substitution for the Name of Yahusha.

IC-XC, **IHS**, and later Chi-Rho and **IXTHUS**, were used to conceal the Name. Let's not adopt their ways.

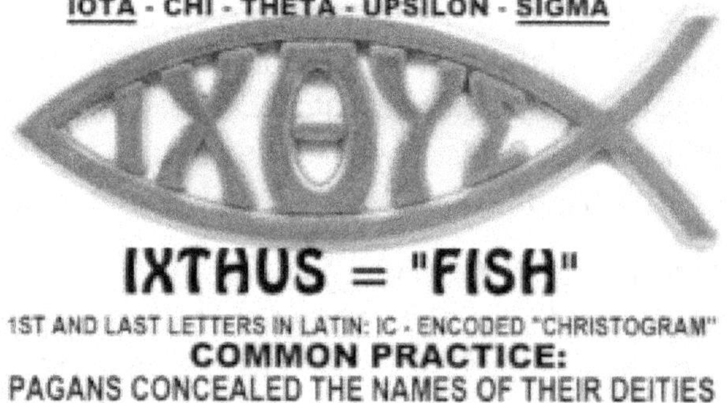

The congregations described in the Natsarim Writings are often described by the Greek term "synagogues" and were not buildings. Even the term "synagogue" helped to make them seem more **gentile** since the word is Greek. The Hebrew term SHUL was avoided. The group may have met in a room, or other place such as Luke described at Acts 16:13 - by a river. The word church (KIRK) originally was a pagan word describing a place of worship. It is seen as kerk, kirk, kirke, circe, circus, cirice. Tyndale used it only twice (Acts 14:13, 19:37) to describe the pagan houses of worship. He was burned at the stake by Henry VIII for his translation, since church referred to the authority (hierarchy) over the laity.

Tyndale used the word *congregation*, making all members of the body on the same level, and not **Nicolaitanes**.

DIVISIONS - LACK OF UNITY

Read Acts 17. Paul goes to the Yahudi assemblies, on a day Luke refers to as the Shabath. The noble Bereans checked Scripture to see if the things Paul said were true. They were not Christians and never became Sun-day observers that ate pigs.

Paul claimed he was a Pharisee, meaning he was brought up in the discipline of the Prushim, one of the strictest sects of them all. After his conversion, Paul was given a new perspective, and unity of the belief in Yahusha's deliverance was his aim; he did not teach against Torah, but established it.

1 Kor. 1:10:

"And I appeal to you, brothers, by the Name of our Master Yahusha Mashiak, that you all agree, and that there be no divisions among you, but that you be knit together in the same mind and in the same opinion."

Paul saw Kefa behaving oddly around the Yahudim when eating with converts from the gentiles, and exposed such hypocrisy to his face (Gal. 2).

Paul realized distortions were coming. From Miletos, Paul called the elders of Ephesus to meet together.

This is what he told them:

"Therefore take heed to yourselves and to all the flock, among which the **Ruach haQodesh** has made you overseers, to shepherd the assembly of Alahim which He has purchased with **His own blood**. For I know this, that after my departure **savage wolves** shall come in among you, not sparing the flock. Also **from among yourselves** men shall arise, speaking distorted teachings, to draw away the talmidim after themselves." Acts 20:28-30 BYNV

Paul's former assignment, when known as *Shaul*, was to arrest those in the congregations who pronounced the Name aloud. This was forbidden, and carried the *death penalty*, since uttering *"Yahuah"* was considered blasphemy.

He watched the robes of the men that stoned Stephen (Acts 7). After meeting Yahusha on the road to Damascus, Paul was proclaiming the true Name, and teaching about Yahusha. Having been arrested, Paul was confronted by the accusations of Tertullus before Felix: **"For having found this man a plague, who stirs up**

dissension among all the Yahudim throughout the world, and a ringleader of the sect of the Natsarim . . ,"

Acts 24:5. Later in this chapter, Paul claims to worship according to all that is written in the Torah and the Prophets. In other words, Paul's way of life was nothing like modern Christianity. He was a "Natsarim," and obeyed the Commandments. The 7th day of the week was still Shabath to him. Paul would not have been shocked about "Sun-day," because he knew *savage wolves* would later come teaching distortions. As savage wolves, they focus on *collecting the tithe,* forsake teaching Torah, and *teaching lawlessness.*

We are witnesses of these distorted teachings, and as Yahusha's **Natsarim** we overthrow them with Truth, in love. ***Pastors are the source of the errors.***

The doctrine one lives by may come from one of two sources: **Scripture** (Yahuah's inspired instructions), or **men's traditions.** Looking around this world, and listening to what is normally taught, it is highly unlikely most people live by what Scripture shows us as pleasing behavior before Yahuah.

Most of our traditions come from pagan sources.

All of these were *inherited from pagans, and not inspired:*

Sun-day assemblies, statues, rosaries, holy water, **Easter** baskets (in place of Passover and First-fruits), Christmas, wreath and tree-decorating, eating swine, sunrise "services" and praying in circles. Another huge stronghold is how everyone is using a false name in place of the true identity of our Deliverer. There is only ***one name*** given among men for deliverance. (see Acts 4:12). Yahusha's Name is *Hebrew.*

The Name is the Stone which the builders rejected (see Psalm, 118). YashaYahu 52:6 tells us Yahuah's people will **know His Name**, Yual (Joel) 2 quoted by Kefa tells us those **calling on it** will be delivered. Acts 4:12 tells us there is one Name.

The Name and the Word are above all else (Ps 138:2), and we Natsarim are the guardians of the Name, and the Word, of Yahuah. What was whispered in the inner rooms is being shouted from the rooftops. If the **Torah of Musheh** is what we are told to ***remember*** before the **Day of Yahuah** comes, then that's what we should be telling everyone (Mal. 4:4-6).

Billions have never even heard the word "**Torah**" in their lives, and yet they support men to teach them the way of deliverance.

The wealth taken away by the Romans under Titus and his father Vespasian was used to build the Roman Colosseum, and build two arches, one for Titus, and one for Vespasian. The arch of Titus still remains, and this photo inside the arch celebrates one of the saddest days for Yerushalayim, which Yahusha foretold.

ARCH OF TITUS

CARVED INSIDE THE ARCH:
THE CELEBRATORY THEFT OF THE GOLDEN MENORAH

Come out of her, My people!
Repent, for the Reign of Yahuah is near!

BYNV SAMPLE TEXT
DANIAL, MALAKI, & NATSARIM INTRODUCTION
The following is a sample text from the BYNV for English readers. Names and places are rendered without the vowel changes of the Masoretes that altered the Eberim phonology after the 8th century CE. *(sect of Qaraitism)*

Get the complete BYNV from Amazon by visiting Lew White's Author's Page.

DANIAL *[My Judge is Alahim]*
DANIAL - AKA: **DANIEL**

1 In the 3rd year of the reign of **Yahuyaqim**, king of Yahudah, **Nebukadnetser**, king of Babel came to Yerushalim and besieged it. ₂And **Yahuah** gave Yahuyaqim king of Yahudah into his hand, with some of the utensils of the House of Alahim, which he brought to the land of Shinar to the house of his mighty one. And he brought the utensils into the treasure house of his mighty one. ₃And the king said to Ashpenaz, the chief of his eunuchs, to bring some of the children of Yisharal and some of the king's descendants and some of the nobles, ₄young men in whom there was no blemish, but good-looking, having insight in all wisdom, having knowledge and capable of learning, equipped to stand in the king's palace, and to teach them the writing and speech of the Kaldeans. ₅And the king appointed for them a daily ration of the king's food and of the wine which he drank, and 3 years of training for them, so that at the end thereof they should stand before the king. ₆Now among them were from the sons of Yahudah: **Danial**, **Kananyah**, **Mishal**, and **Azaryah**. ₇And the chief of the **eunuchs** gave them names. For he called Danial, Belteshatsar; and Kananyah, Shadrak; and Mishaal, Meyshak; and Azaryah, Abed-Nego. *[likely, they were made eunuchs]* ₈But Danial laid it upon his heart that he would not defile himself with the portion of the king's food, nor with the wine which he drank. So he asked from the chief of the eunuchs not to defile himself. ₉And Alahim granted Danial kindness and compassion from the chief of the eunuchs, ₁₀but the chief of the eunuchs said to Danial, "I fear my Aduni the king, who has appointed your food and drink. For why should he see your faces looking worse than the young men who are your age? Then you would make my head guilty before the king!" ₁₁And Danial said to the overseer whom the chief of the eunuchs had set over Danial, Kananyah, Mishal, and Azaryah, ₁₂"Please try your servants for 10 Yomim, and let them give us vegetables to eat and water to drink. ₁₃Then let our appearances be examined before you, and the appearances of the young men who eat the portion of the king's food. And do with your servants as you see fit." ₁₄And he listened to them in this matter, and tried them 10 Yomim. ₁₅And at the end of 10 Yomim their appearances looked better and fatter in flesh than all the young men who ate the portion of the king's food. ₁₆And it came to be that the overseer took away their portion of food and the wine they were to drink, and gave them vegetables. ₁₇As for these 4 young men, Alahim gave them knowledge and skill in all learning and wisdom. And Danial had understanding in all visions and dreams. ₁₈And at the end of the Yomim, when the king had said that they should be brought in, the chief of the eunuchs brought them in before Nebukadnetser. ₁₉And the king spoke with them, and none among them all were found like Danial, Kananyah, Mishal, and Azaryah, so they stood before the king. ₂₀And in any word of wisdom and understanding about which the king examined them, he found them 10 times better than all the magicians, the astrologers, who were in all his reign. 21And Danial continued until the 1st year of King **Koresh**.

DANIAL - AKA: **DANIEL**

2 And in the 2nd year of the reign of Nebukadnetser, Nebukadnetser had dreams. And his ruach was so troubled that his sleep left him. 2And the king gave orders to call the magicians, and the astrologers, and the practicers of witchcraft, and the Kaldeans to declare to the king his dreams. So they came and stood before the king. 3And the king said to them, "I have had a dream, and my ruach is troubled to know the dream." 4And the Kaldeans spoke to the king in Aramaic, "O king, live forever! Relate the dream to your servants, and we shall reveal the interpretation." 5The king answered and said to the Kaldeans, "My decision is firm: if you do not make known the dream and its interpretation to me, your limbs shall be taken from you, and your houses made dunghills. 6But if you reveal the dream and its interpretation, you shall receive gifts, and rewards, and great esteem from me. So reveal to me the dream and its interpretation." 7They answered again and said, "Let the king relate to his servants the dream, and we shall reveal its interpretation." 8The king answered and said, "I know for certain that you would gain time, because you see that my decision is firm: 9If you do not make known the dream to me, there is only one decree for you! For you have agreed to speak lying and corrupt words before me till the time has changed. So relate the dream to me, then I shall know that you shall reveal its interpretation for me." 10The Kaldeans answered the king, and said, "There is no one on arets who is able to reveal the matter of the king. Because no king, Aduni, or ruler has ever asked a matter like this of any magician, or astrologer, or Kaldean. 11And the matter that the king is asking is difficult, and there is no other who is able to reveal it to the king except the Alahin, whose dwelling is not with flesh." 12Because of this the king was enraged and very angry, and gave orders to destroy all the wise ones of Babel. 13So the decree went out, and they began killing the wise ones. And they sought Danial and his companions, to kill them. 14Then with counsel and wisdom Danial answered Aryok, the chief of the king's guard, who had gone out to kill the wise ones of Babel – 15he answered and said to Aryok the king's officer, "Why is the decree from the king so urgent?" So Aryok made the decision known to Danial. 16And Danial went in and asked the king to give him time, and he would show the king the interpretation. 17Then Danial went to his house, and made the decision known to Kananyah, Mishal, and Azaryah, his companions, 18 to seek compassion from the Alah of the shamayim concerning this secret, so that Danial and his companions should not perish with the rest of the wise ones of Babel. 19Then the secret was revealed to Danial in a lailah vision, and Danial blessed the Alah of the shamayim. 20Danial responded and said, "Blessed be the Name of Alah forever and ever, for wisdom and might are His. 21And He changes the times and the seasons. He removes kings and raises up kings. He gives wisdom to the wise and knowledge to those who possess understanding. 22He reveals deep and secret things. He knows what is in the darkness, and light dwells with Him. 23I thank You and praise You, Alah of my fathers. You have given me wisdom and might, and have now made known to me what we asked of You, for You have made known to us the king's matter." 24So Danial went to Aryok, whom the king had appointed to destroy the wise ones of Babel. He went and said this to him, "Do not destroy the wise ones of Babel. Bring me in before the king, and I shall show the interpretation to the king." 25Then Aryok brought Danial in a hurry before the king, and said thus to him, "I have found a man among the sons of the exile of Yahudah, who does make known to the king the interpretation." 26The king answered and said to Danial, whose name was Belteshatsar, "Are you able to make known to me the dream which I have seen, and its interpretation?" 27Danial answered before the king, and said, "The secret which the king is

asking – the wise ones, the astrologers, the magicians, and the diviners are unable to show it to the king. 28But there is an Alah in the shamayim who reveals secrets, and He has made known to King Nebukadnetser what is to be in the latter Yomim. Your dream, and the visions of your head upon your bed, were these: 29As for you, king, on your bed your thoughts came up: What is going to take place after this. And He who reveals secrets has made known to you what shall be; 30As for me, this secret has not been revealed to me because I have more wisdom than anyone living, but for our sakes who make known the interpretation to the king, and that you should know the thoughts of your heart. 31You, king, were looking on, and saw a great image! This great image, and its shining excellent, was standing before you, and its form was awesome. 32This image's **head** was of fine gold, its **chest and arms** of silver, its **belly and thighs** of bronze, 33its **legs** of iron, its **feet** partly of iron and partly of clay. 34You were looking on, until a **Stone** was cut out without hands, and it smote the image on its feet of iron and clay, and broke them in pieces. 35Then the iron, the clay, the bronze, the silver, and the gold were crushed together, and became like chaff from the summer threshing-floors. And the wind took them away so that no trace of them was found. And the Stone that smote the image became a great mountain and filled all the arets. 36This is the dream, and its interpretation we declare before the king. 37You, king, are a king of kings. For the Alah of the shamayim has given you a reign, power, and strength, and preciousness, 38and wherever the children of men dwell, or the beasts of the field and the birds of the shamayim, He has given them into your hand, and has made you ruler over them all. You are the head of gold. 39And after you rises up another reign lower than yours, and another 3rd reign of bronze that rules over all the arets. 40And the **4th reign is as strong as iron**, because iron crushes and shatters all. So, like iron that breaks in pieces, it crushes and breaks all these." *[Rome through the Uniting of all Guyim, NWO?]* 41"Yet, as you saw the feet and toes, partly of potter's clay and partly of iron, the reign is to be divided. But some of the strength of the iron is to be in it, because you saw the iron mixed with muddy clay. 42And as the toes of the feet were partly of iron and partly of clay, so the reign is partly strong and partly brittle. 43And as you saw iron mixed with muddy clay, they are mixing themselves with the seed of men, but they are not clinging to each other, even as iron does not mix with clay. 44And in the Yomim of these kings the Alah of the shamayim shall set up a reign which shall never be destroyed, nor the reign pass on to other people – it crushes and puts to an end all these reigns, and it shall stand forever. 45Because you saw that the Stone was cut out of the mountain without hands, and that it crushed the iron, the bronze, the clay, the silver, and the gold, the great Alah has made known to the king what shall be after this. And the dream is true, and its interpretation is trustworthy." 46Then King Nebukadnetser fell on his face, and did obeisance before Danial, and gave orders to present to him an offering and incense. 47The king answered Danial, and said, "Truly your Alah is the Alah of alahin, Aduni of kings, and a revealer of secrets, since you were able to reveal this secret." 48Then the king made Danial great and gave him many great gifts, and made him ruler over all the province of Babel, and chief of the nobles, over all the wise ones of Babel. 49And Danial asked of the king, and he set Shadrak, Meyshak, and Abed- Nego over the work of the province of Babel, and Danial in the gate of the king.

DANIAL - AKA: **DANIEL**

3 Nebukadnetser the king made a **tselem** *[image]* of gold, whose height was 60 cubits and its width 6 cubits. He set it up in the plain of Dura, in the province of Babel. 2And King Nebukadnetser sent word to gather together the viceroys, the nobles, and the governors, the counsellors, the treasurers, the judges, the magistrates, and all the officials of the provinces, to come to the dedication of the image which King Nebukadnetser had set

up. ₃Then the viceroys, the nobles, and the governors, the counsellors, the treasurers, the judges, the magistrates, and all the officials of the provinces gathered together for the dedication of the image that King Nebukadnetser had set up. And they stood before the image that Nebukadnetser had set up. ₄Then a herald loudly proclaimed, "To you it is commanded, O peoples, Guyim, and languages, ₅that **as soon as you hear the sound** of the horn, the flute, the zither, the lyre, the harp, the pipes, and all kinds of instruments *[playing the anthem]*, you shall **fall down** and do **obeisance to the gold image** that King Nebukadnetser has set up. ₆And whoever does not fall down and do obeisance is immediately thrown into the midst of a burning furnace of fire." ₇So as soon as all the people heard the sound of the horn, the flute, the zither, the lyre, the harp, all kinds of instruments, all the people, Guyim, and languages fell down and did obeisance to the gold image that King Nebukadnetser had set up. ₈Thereupon, at that time, certain Kaldeans came forward and accused the Yahudim. ₉They spoke and said to King Nebu- kadnetsar, "O king, live forever! ₁₀"You, O king, have made a decree that **everyone who hears the sound** of the horn, the flute, the zither, the lyre, the harp, the pipes, and all kinds of instruments, **shall fall down and do obeisance to the gold image,** ₁₁and whoever does not fall down and do obeisance is thrown into the midst of a burning furnace of fire. ₁₂There are certain Yahudim whom you have set over the work of the province of Babel: Shadrak, Meyshak, and Abed- Nego. These men, O king, pay no heed to you. They do not serve your alahin, and they are not doing obeisance to the gold image which you have set up." ₁₃Then Nebukadnetser, in rage and wrath, gave orders to bring Shadrak, Meyshak, and Abed-Nego. Then they brought these men before the king. ₁₄Nebukadnetser spoke and said to them, "Is it true, Shadrak, Meyshak, and Abed-Nego, that you do not serve my alahin, and you do not do obeisance to the gold image which I have set up? ₁₅"Now if you are ready when you hear the sound of the horn, the flute, the zither, the lyre, the harp, the pipes, and all kinds of instruments, and you fall down and do obeisance to the image which I have made, good! But if you do not do obeisance, you are immediately thrown into the midst of a burning furnace of fire. And who is the alah who does deliver you from my hands?" ₁₆Shadrak, Meyshak, and Abed-Nego answered and said to the king, "O Nebukadnetser, we have no need to answer you in this matter. ₁₇"For if so, our Alah whom we serve is able to deliver us from the burning furnace of fire and from your hand, king – He does deliver! ₁₈But if not, let it be known to you, king, that we do not serve your elahin, nor do we do obeisance to the gold image which you have set up." ₁₉Then Nebukadnetser was filled with wrath, and the expression on his face changed toward Shadrak, Meyshak, and Abed-Nego. He responded and gave orders that they heat the furnace 7 times more than it was usual to heat it. ₂₀And he commanded some of the strongest men of his army to bind Shadrak, Meyshak, and Abed-Nego, and throw them into the burning furnace of fire. ₂₁So these men were bound in their coats, their trousers, and their turbans, and their other garments, and were thrown into the midst of the burning furnace of fire. ₂₂Thereupon, because the king's order was urgent, and the furnace exceedingly hot, the flame of the fire killed those men who took up Shadrak, Meyshak, and Abed-Nego. ₂₃And these three men, Shadrak, Meyshak, and Abed-Nego, fell down bound into the midst of the burning furnace of fire. ₂₄Then King Nebukadnetser was amazed, and stood up in haste and spoke and said to his counsellors, "Did we not throw 3 men bound into the midst of the fire?" They answered and said to the king, "Certainly, O king." ₂₅He answered and said, "Look! I see **4 men** loose, walking in the midst of the fire. And they are not hurt, and the form of **the 4th is like the Son of Alah."** ₂₆Then Nebukadnetser went near the mouth of the burning furnace of fire. He spoke and said, "Shadrak, Meyshak, and Abed-Nego, servants of the Highest One Alah, come out, and come here." Then Shadrak, Meyshak, and Abed-Nego came from the midst of the fire. ₂₇And the viceroys, the nobles, and the governors, and the king's counselors gathered together, seeing these men on whose bodies the fire had no power, and the hair of their head was not singed nor were their garments changed, nor did the smell of fire come on them. 28Nebukadnetser responded and said, "Blessed be the Alah of Shadrak, Meyshak, and Abed-Nego, who sent His Messenger and delivered His servants who trusted in Him, and changed the king's order, and gave up their bodies, that they should not serve nor do obeisance to any alah except their own Alah! 29Therefore I make a decree that whoever of any people, nation, or language who speaks any lawless against the Alah of Shadrak, Meyshak, and Abed-Nego, his limbs shall be taken, and his house made a dunghill, because there is no other Alah who is able to deliver like this." 30Then the king promoted Shadrak, Meyshak, and Abed-Nego in the province of Babel.

DANIAL - AKA: **DANIEL**

4 Nebukadnetser the king, to all peoples, Guyim and languages that dwell in all the arets: Peace be increased to you. 2I thought it good to declare the signs and wonders which the Highest One Alah has worked for me. 3How great are His signs, and how mighty His wonders! His reign is an everlasting reign, and His rulership is from generation to generation. 4I, Nebukadnetser, was at rest in my house, and prospering in my palace. 5I saw a dream and it frightened me, and the thoughts on my bed and the visions of my head alarmed me. 6So I issued a decree to bring in all the wise ones of Babel before me, to make known to me the interpretation of the dream. 7So the magicians, the astrologers, the Kaldeans, and the diviners came in, and I related the dream to them, but its interpretation they did not make known to me. 8And at last Danial, whose name is Belteshatsar, according to the name of my alah, came before me. In him is the Ruach of the Qodesh Alah. So I related the dream to him, saying, 9"Belteshatsar, chief of the magicians, because I know that the Ruach of the qodesh Alah is in you, and no secret is too difficult for you, explain to me the visions of my dream that I have seen, and its interpretation. 10Now the visions of my head on my bed were these: I looked, and saw a tree in the midst of the arets, and its height great. 11The tree became great and strong, and its height reached to the shamayim, and it was visible to the ends of all the arets. 12Its leaves were lovely, and its fruit plenty, and in it was food for all. The beasts of the field found shade under it, and the birds of the shamayim dwelt in its branches, and all flesh was fed from it. 13In the visions of my head on my bed, I looked and saw a Watcher, even a qodesh one, coming down from the shamayim. 14He cried aloud and said this, 'Hew down the tree and cut off its branches, strip off its leaves and scatter its fruit. Let the beasts flee from under it, and the birds from its branches. 15But leave the stump of its roots in the arets, even with a band of iron and bronze, in the tender grass of the field. And let it be wet with the dew of the shamayim, and let his portion be with the beasts on the grass of the arets. 16Let his heart be changed from man's, let him be given the heart of a **beast**, and 7 times pass over him. 17This matter is by the decree of the watchers, and the command by the word of the qodesh ones, so that the living know that the Highest One is ruler in the reign of men, and gives it to whomever He wishes, **and sets over it the lowest of men**.' 18This dream have I seen, I, King Nebukadnetser. And you, Belteshatsar, reveal its interpretation, since all the wise ones of my reign are unable to make known to me the interpretation. But you are able, for the Ruach of the Qodesh Alah is in you." 19Then Danial, whose name was Belteshatsar, was stunned for a short time, and his thoughts alarmed him. The king responded and said, "Belteshatsar, do not let the dream or its interpretation alarm you." Belteshatsar answered and said, "My Aduni, the dream is to those who hate you, and its interpretation to your enemies! 20The tree you saw, which became great and strong, whose height reached to the shamayim and was

visible to all the arets, 21whose leaves were lovely and its fruit plenty, and in it was food for all, under which the beasts of the field dwelt, and on whose branches the birds of the shamayim sat – 22it is you, O king, for you have become great and strong. And your greatness has grown, and has reached to the shamayim and your rulership to the end of the arets. 23And as the king saw a Watcher, even a qodesh one, coming down from the shamayim, and he said, 'Hew down the tree and destroy it, but leave the stump of its roots in the arets, even with a band of iron and bronze in the tender grass of the field. And let it be wet with the dew of the shamayim, and let his portion be with the beasts of the field, till seven times pass over him' – 24this is the interpretation, king, and this is the decree of the Highest One, which has come upon my Aduni the king: 25That you are going to be driven away from men, and your dwelling be with the beasts of the field, and you be given grass to eat like oxen, and you be wetted with the dew of the shamayim, and 7 times pass over you, till you know that the Highest One is ruler in the reign of men, and that He gives it to whomever He wishes. 26And they that gave the command to leave the stump of its roots of the tree: your reign remains yours, from the time you come to know that the shamayim are ruling. 27Therefore, O king, let my counsel be acceptable to you, and break off your sins by obedience, and your lawlessnesses by showing favor to the poor – your prosperity might be extended." 28All this came upon King Nebu- kadnetsar. 29At the end of the 12 months he was walking about the palace of the reign of Babel. 30The king spoke and said, "Is not this great Babel, which I myself have built, for the house of the reign, by the might of **my power** and for the esteem of **my splendor**?" 31The word was still in the king's mouth, when a voice fell from the shamayim, "King Nebukadnetser, to you it is spoken: the reign has been taken away from you, 32and you are driven away from men, and your dwelling is to be with the beasts of the field. You are given grass to eat like oxen, and 7 times shall pass over you, until you know that the Highest One is ruler in the reign of men, and He gives it to whomever He wishes." 33In that hour the word was executed on Nebukadnetser, and he was driven from men and he ate grass like oxen, and his body was wet with the dew of the shamayim till his hair had grown like eagles' *feathers* and his nails like birds' *claws*. 34And at the end of the Yomim I, Nebukadnetser, lifted my eyes to the shamayim, and my understanding returned to me. And I blessed the Highest One and praised and made Him great who lives forever, Whose rule is an everlasting rule, and His reign is from generation to generation. 35And all the inhabitants of the arets are of no account, and He does as He wishes with the host of the shamayim and among the inhabitants of the arets. And there is none to strike against His hand or say to Him, "What have You done?" 36At the same time my understanding returned to me, and for the preciousness of my reign, my esteem and splendor were returning to me. And my counselors and nobles sought me out, and I was reestablished to my reign, and excellent greatness was added to me. 37Now I, Nebukadnetser, am praising and exalting and esteeming the King of the shamayim, for all His works are truth, and His ways right. **And those who walk in pride He is able to humble**.

[My Judge is Alahim]

DANIAL

DANIAL - AKA: **DANIEL**

5 **Belshatsar** the king made a great feast for 1,000 of his great men, and drank wine in the presence of the thousand. 2While tasting the wine, Belshatstsar gave orders to bring the gold and silver vessels which his father Nebukadnetser had taken from the Hekal which had been in Yerushalim, that the king and his great men, his wives, and his concubines could drink from them. ₃Then they brought the gold vessels that had been taken from the Hekal of the House of Alah which had been in Yerushalim. And the king and his great men, his wives, and his concubines drank out of them. ₄They drank wine, and praised the elahin of gold, and of silver, of bronze, of iron, of wood and of stone. ₅At that moment the **fingers** of a man's hand appeared and wrote opposite the lampstand on the plaster of the wall of the king's palace. And the king saw the part of the hand that wrote. ₆Then the king's colour changed, and his thoughts alarmed him, so that the joints of his hips were loosened and his knees knocked against each other. ₇The king screamed loudly to bring in the astrologers, the Kaldeans, and the diviners. The king spoke and said to the wise ones of Babel, "Whoever reads this writing, and shows me its interpretation, is robed in purple and has a chain of gold around his neck, and shall be the 3rd ruler in the reign." ₈So all the king's wise ones came, but they were unable to read the writing, or to make known its interpretation to the king. ₉Then King Belshatsar was greatly alarmed, and his colour changed, and his great men were puzzled. ₁₀The empress, because of the words of the king and his great men, came to the banquet hall. And the empress spoke and said, "O king, live forever! Do not let your thoughts alarm you, nor let your colour change. ₁₁There is a man in your reign in whom is the Ruach of the Qodesh Alah. And in the Yomim of your father, light and understanding and wisdom, like the wisdom of the Alahin, were found in him. And King Nebukadnetser your father, your father the king, made him chief of the magicians, astrologers, Kaldeans, and diviners, ₁₂because an excellent ruach, knowledge and understanding, interpreting dreams, and explaining riddles, and solving difficult problems were found in this **Danial**, whom the king named **Belteshatsar** [Beltis Protects]. Now let Danial be called, and let him show the interpretation." ₁₃So Danial was brought in before the king. The king spoke and said to Danial, "Are you that Danial who is one of the sons of the exile from Yahudah, whom my father the king brought from Yahudah? ₁₄I have heard of you, that the Ruach of Elah is in you, and that light and understanding and excellent wisdom are found in you. ₁₅And the wise ones, the astrologers, have been brought in before me, that they should read this writing and make known to me its interpretation, but they were unable to show the interpretation of the word. ₁₆And I myself have heard of you, that you are able to give interpretations and to solve difficult problems. Now if you are able to read the writing and make known its interpretation to me, you are to be robed in purple and have a chain of gold around your neck, and shall be the 3rd ruler in the reign." ₁₇Then Danial answered and said before the king, "Let your gifts be for yourself, and give your rewards to another. Yet I shall read the writing to the king, and make known the interpretation to him. ₁₈ King, the Highest One Alah gave Nebukadnetser your father a reign and greatness, and preciousness and esteem. ₁₉ And because of the greatness which He gave him, all peoples, Guyim, and languages trembled and feared before him. Whomever he wished he executed, and whomever he wished he kept alive, and whomever he wished he raised up, and whomever he wished he made low. ₂₀But when his heart was lifted up, and his ruach was so strong as to act proudly, he was put down from his throne of reign, and they took his preciousness from him. ₂₁Then he was driven from the sons of men, and his heart was made like the beasts, and his dwelling was with the wild donkeys. He was given grass to eat like oxen, and his body was wet with the dew of the shamayim, till he knew that the Highest One Alah is ruler in the reign of men, and He sets up over it whomever He wishes. ₂₂And you his son, **Belshatsar** [Bel protects; – he was the last king of Babel], have not humbled your heart, **although you knew all this.** ₂₃And you have lifted yourself up against Aduni of the shamayim. And they brought before you the vessels of His House, and you and your great men, your wives and your concubines, have been drinking wine from them. And **you have praised the alahin of silver, and of gold, of bronze, of iron, of wood, and of stone**, which neither see nor hear nor know. **But the Alah Who holds your breath in His hand and owns all your ways, you have not made**

great. 24Then the part of the hand was sent from Him, and this writing was inscribed. 25And this is the writing that was inscribed: **MENE MENE TEQEL UPARSIN** 26 "This is the interpretation of each word: MENE – Alah has numbered your reign, and put an end to it. 27TEQEL – You have been weighed on the scales, and found lacking. 28PERES – Your reign has been divided, and given to the Medes and Persians." 29Then Belshatsar gave orders, and they robed Danial in purple and put a chain of gold around his neck, and they proclaimed concerning him that he is the 3rd ruler in the reign. 30In that lailah Belshatsar, king of the Kaldeans, was slain. 31And **Daryush** the Mede took over the reign, being about 62 years old.

MINA   MINA   TEKAL   UPARSIN

ᎩᏃᎨᎮᎷᎩᎩ   ᏞᏏᎭ   ᎭᏃᎷ   ᎭᏃᎷ

UPARSIN   TEKAL   MINA   MINA

DANIAL - AKA: **DANIEL**

6 It pleased Daryush to appoint over the reign 120 viceroys, to be over all the reign, 2and over them 3 governors, of whom Danial was one, so that these viceroys should give account to them, and the king suffer no loss. 3Then this Danial distinguished himself above the governors and viceroys, because an excellent ruach was in him. And the king planned to appoint him over all the reign. 4Then the governors and viceroys sought to find occasion against Danial concerning the reign. But they were unable to find occasion or corruption, because he was steadfast, and no negligence or corruption was found in him. 5Then these men said, "We shall not find any occasion against this Danial unless we find it against him concerning the law of his Alah." 6Then these governors and viceroys tumultuously gathered before the king, and said this to him, "King Daryush, live forever! 7"All the governors of the reign, the nobles and viceroys, the counsellors and advisors, have consulted together to establish a royal decree and to make a strong interdict, that whoever petitions any alah or man for 30 Yomim, except you, O king, is thrown into the den of lions. 8Now, O king, establish the interdict and sign the writing, so that it is not to be changed, according to the law of the Medes and Persians, which does not pass away." 9So King Daryush signed the written interdict. 10And Danial, when he knew that the writing was signed, went home and in his upper room with his windows open toward Yerushalim he knelt down on his knees 3 times per yom, and prayed and gave thanks before his Alah, as he had done before. 11Then these men tumultuously gathered and found Danial praying and entreating before his Alah. 12Then they approached the king, and spoke concerning the king's interdict, "Have you not signed a interdict that every man who petitions any alah or man within 30 Yomim, except you, O king, is thrown into the den of lions?" The king answered and said, "The word is certain, according to the law of the Medes and Persians, which does not pass away." 13Then they answered and said before the king, "Danial, who is one of the sons of the exile from Yahudah, pays no heed to you, O king, nor for the interdict that you have signed, but makes his petition 3 times per yom." 14Then the king, when he heard these words, was greatly displeased with himself, and set his heart on Danial to deliver him. And he labored till the going down of the sun to deliver him. 15Then these men tumultuously gathered before the king, and said to the king, "Know, O king, that it is the law of the Medes and Persians that any interdict or decree which the king establishes is not to be changed." 16Then the king gave orders, and they brought Danial and threw him into the den of lions. But the king spoke and said to Danial, "Your Alah, whom you serve continually, He Himself delivers you." 17And a stone was brought and laid on the mouth of the den, and the king sealed it with his own signet and with the signets of his great men, that the situation concerning Danial might not be changed. ₁₈And the king went to his palace and spent the lailah fasting. And no entertainment was brought before him, and his sleep fled from him. ₁₉Then the king rose up very early in the morning and hurried to the den of lions. ₂₀And when he came to the den, he called with a grieved voice to Danial. The king spoke and said to Danial, "Danial, servant of the living Alah, has your Alah, whom you serve continually, been able to deliver you from the lions?" ₂₁Then Danial said to the king, "O king, live forever! ₂₂My Alah has sent His messenger and has shut the lions' mouths, and they did not harm me, because I was found innocent before Him. And also before you, O king, I have done no harm." ₂₃Then the king was very glad and gave orders that Danial be taken up out of the den. And Danial was taken up out of the den, and no harm was found on him, because he trusted in his Alah. ₂₄And the king gave orders and they brought those men who had accused Danial, and they threw them, their children, and their wives into the den of lions. And the lions overpowered them, and broke all their bones in pieces before they reached the floor of the den. ₂₅Then King Daryush wrote to all peoples, Guyim, and languages that dwell in all the arets: "Peace be increased to you. ₂₆From before me is made a decree that throughout every rule of my reign men are to tremble and fear before the Alah of Danial, for He is the living Alah, and steadfast forever. And His reign is one which is not destroyed, and His rule is to the end. ₂₇He delivers and rescues, and He works signs and wonders in the shamayim and on arets, for He has delivered Danial from the power of the lions." ₂₈And this Danial prospered in the reign of Daryush and in the reign of Koresh the Persian.

DANIAL - AKA: **DANIEL**

7 In the 1st year of Belshatsar king of Babel, Danial had a dream and visions of his head on his bed. Then he wrote down the dream, giving a summary of the matters. ₂Danial spoke and said, "I was looking in my vision by lailah and saw the 4 winds of the shamayim stirring up the Great Sea. ₃And **4** great **beasts** came up from the sea, different from one another. ₄The 1st was like a **lion**, and had eagle's wings. I was looking until its wings were plucked off, and it was lifted up from the arets and made to stand on 2 feet like a man, and it was given a man's heart. ₅And see, another beast, a 2nd, like a **bear**. And it was raised up on one side, and had 3 ribs in its mouth between its teeth. And they said this to it, 'Arise,devour much flesh!' ₆After this I looked and saw another, like a **leopard**, which had on its back 4 wings of a bird. The beast also had 4 heads, and rule was given to it. ₇After this I looked in the lailah visions and saw a **4th beast**, fearsome and burly, exceedingly strong. And it had great iron teeth. It devoured and crushed, and trampled down the rest with its feet. And it was different from all the beasts that were before it, and it had **10 horns**. ₈I was thinking about the horns, then saw another horn, a little one, coming up among them, and three of the first horns were plucked out by the roots before it. And see, **eyes like the eyes of a man** were in this horn, and a mouth speaking great *words*. ₉I was looking until thrones were set up, and the **Ancient of Yomim** was seated. [Attiq Yomin, Ancient of Days] His garment was white as snow, and the hair of His head was like clean wool, His throne was flames of fire, its wheels burning fire. ₁₀A stream of fire was flowing and coming forth from His presence, and 1,000 thousands served Him, and 10,000 times 10,000 stood before Him, the Judge was seated, and the books were opened. ₁₁I was looking. Then, because of the sound of the great words which the **horn** was speaking, I was looking until the beast was slain, and its **body** destroyed and **given to the burning fire**, ₁₂ and the rest of the beasts had their rule taken away. But a lengthening of life was given to them, for a season and a time. ₁₃I was looking in the lailah visions and saw **One like the Son of Anush** [Man] **coming with the clouds of the shamayim!** And He came to the Ancient of Yomim, and they brought Him near before Him. ₁₄And to Him was given rulership

and preciousness and a reign, that all peoples, Guyim, and languages should serve Him. His rule is an everlasting rule which shall not pass away, and His reign that which shall not be destroyed. ₁₅"As for me, Danial, my ruach was pierced within my body, and the visions of my head alarmed me. ₁₆I drew near to one of those who stood by, and asked him the certainty of all this. And he spoke to me and made known to me the interpretation of the matters: ₁₇'These great beasts, which are 4, are 4 kings which rise up from the arets. ₁₈Then the qodesh ones of the Most High shall receive the reign, and possess the reign forever, even forever and ever.' ₁₉Then I desired for certainty concerning the **4th beast**, which was different from all the others, very fearsome, with its teeth of iron and its nails of bronze, which devoured, crushed, and trampled down the rest with its feet, ₂₀and concerning the 10 horns that were on its head, and of the other *horn* that came up, before which three fell – this horn which had eyes and a mouth which spoke great *words*, whose appearance was greater than his fellows. ₂₁I was looking, and **this horn was fighting against the qodesh ones**, and was prevailing against them, ₂₂until the Ancient of Yomim came, and lawfulness was given to the qodesh ones of the Highest One, and the time came **and the qodesh ones took possession of the reign.** ₂₃"This is what he said, 'The **4th beast** is the 4th reign on arets, which is different from all other reigns, and **it devours all the arets**, tramples it down and crushes it. *[All history has seen separate kingdoms, each given borders set by Yahuah. In the last days, a global one-world power is set up to devour all reigns, with 10 "territories" over Earth. This is the work of the Planners, to set up a New World Order aka New Age, under the United Guyim]* ₂₄'And the ten horns are ten kings from this reign. They shall rise, and another shall rise after them, and it is different from the first ones, and it humbles three kings, ₂₅and it speaks words against the Most High, and it wears out the qodesh ones of the Highest One, and it intends to change appointed times and Turah, and they are given into its hand for a time and times and half a time. ₂₆But the Judgement shall sit, and they shall take away its rule, to cut off and to destroy, until the end. ₂₇And the reign, and the rulership, and the greatness of the reigns under all the shamayim, shall be given to the people, the qodesh ones of the Highest One. His reign is an everlasting reign, and all rulerships shall serve and obey Him.' ₂₈This is the end of the matter. As for me, Danial, my thoughts greatly alarmed me, and my colour changed. And I kept the matter in my heart."

DANIAL - AKA: **DANIEL**

8 In the 3rd year of the reign of Belshatsar the king, a vision appeared to me, Danial, after the one that appeared to me the first time. ₂And I looked in the vision, and it came to be while I was looking, that I was in the citadel of **Shushan**, which is in the province of Eylam. And I looked in the vision, and I was by the River Ulai. ₃And I lifted my eyes and looked and saw a ram standing beside the river, and it had 2 horns, and the 2 horns were high. And the one was higher than the other, and the higher one came up last. ₄I saw the ram pushing westward, and northward, and southward, so that no beast could stand before him, and there was no one to deliver from his hand, while he did as he pleased and became great. ₅And I was observing and saw a male goat came from the west, over the surface of all the arets, without touching the ground. And the goat had a conspicuous horn between his eyes. ₆And he came to the ram that had 2 horns, which I had seen standing beside the river, and ran at him in the rage of his power. ₇And I saw him come close to the ram, and he became embittered against him, and smote the ram, and broke his 2 horns. And there was no power in the ram to withstand him, but he threw him down to the ground and trampled on him. And there was no one to deliver the ram from his hand. ₈And the male goat became very great. But when he was strong, the large horn was broken, and in place of it 4 conspicuous ones came up toward the 4 winds of the shamayim. ₉And from one of them came a little horn which became exceedingly great toward the south, and toward the east, and toward the Splendid *Land*. ₁₀And it became great, up to the host of the shamayim. And it caused some of the host and some of the stars to fall to the arets, and trampled them down. ₁₁It even exalted itself as high as the Prince of the host. And it took that which is continual away from Him, and threw down the foundation of His qodesh place. ₁₂And because of transgression, an army was given over *to the horn* to oppose that which is continual. And it threw the Truth down to the ground, and it acted and prospered. ₁₃Then I heard a certain qodesh one speaking. And another qodesh one said to that certain one who was speaking, "Till when is the vision, concerning that which is continual, and the transgression that lays waste, to make both the qodesh place and the host to be trampled under foot?" ₁₄And he said to me, "For 2,300 Yomim (evenings and mornings), then that which is qodesh shall be made right." ₁₅And it came to be, when I, Danial, had seen the vision, that I sought understanding, and see, before me stood one having the appearance of a mighty man. ₁₆And I heard a man's voice between *the banks of* Ulai, who called, and said, "**Gabrial**, make this man understand the vision." ₁₇He then came near where I stood. And when he came I feared and I fell on my face, but he said to me, **"Understand, son of man, for the vision is for the time of the end."** ₁₈And, as he was speaking with me, I fell stunned upon my face to the ground, but he touched me, and made me stand up straight, ₁₉and said, "Look, I am making known to you what shall take place in the latter time of the wrath, for at the appointed time shall be the end. ₂₀The ram which you saw, having two horns, are the kings of Media and Persia. ₂₁And the male goat is the king of Yun *[Greece]*, and the large horn between its eyes is the first king. *[Alexander]* ₂₂And that it was broken and 4 stood up in its place: are 4 rulerships arising out of that nation, but not in its power. ₂₃And in the latter time of their rule, when the transgressors have filled up their measure, a king, fierce of face and skilled at intrigues, shall stand up. ₂₄And his power shall be mighty, but not by his own power, and he shall destroy incredibly, and shall prosper and thrive, and destroy mighty men, and the qodesh people. ₂₅And through his skill he shall make **deceit prosper** in his hand, and hold himself to be great in his heart, and destroy many who are at ease, and even stand against the Prince of princes – yet without hand he shall be broken. ₂₆And what was said in the vision of the evenings and mornings is truth. And hide the vision, for it is after many Yomim." ₂₇And I, Danial, was stricken and became sick for Yomim. Then I rose up and went about the king's work. And I was amazed at the vision, but there was no understanding.

DANIAL - AKA: **DANIEL**

9 In the first year of Daryush the son of Akashurush, of the seed of the Medes, who was set up as king over the reign of the Kaldeans – ₂ in the first year of his reign I, Danial, observed from the Scriptures the number of the years, according to the word of **Yahuah** given to **Yirmeyah** the prophet, for the completion of the wastes of Yerushalim would be **70 years**. ₃So I set my face toward **Yahuah** the Alahim to seek by prayer and supplications, with fasting, and sackcloth, and ashes. ₄And I prayed to **Yahuah** my Alahim, and made admition, and said, "**Yahuah**, great and awesome Al, guarding the Covenant and the kindness to those who love Him, and to those who guard His commands. ₅We have sinned and did lawlessness, and did lawless and rebelled, to turn aside from Your commands and from Your directives. ₆And we have not listened to Your servants the prophets, who spoke in Your Name to our kings, our heads, and our fathers, and to all the people of the land. ₇ **Yahuah**, to You is the obedience, and to us the **shame of face**, as it is this yom – to the men of Yahudah, to the inhabitants of Yerushalim and all Yisharal, those near and those far off in all the lands to which You have driven them, because of their trespass which they have trespassed against

You. ₈"Adoni, to us is the **shame of face**, to our kings, to our heads, and to our fathers, because we have sinned against You. ₉To **Yahuah** our Alahim are the compassions and forgivenesses, for we have rebelled against Him. ₁₀"And we have not obeyed the voice of **Yahuah** our Alahim, to walk in His Turoth, which He set before us through His servants the prophets. ₁₁And all Yisharal have transgressed Your Turah, and turned aside, so as not to obey Your voice. So the curse and the oath written in the Turah of Mushah the servant of Alahim have been poured out on us, for we have sinned against Him. ₁₂And He has confirmed His words, which He spoke against us and against our rulers who judged us, by bringing upon us great evil. For under all the shamayim there has not been done like what was done to Yerushalim. ₁₃As it is written in the Turah of Mushah, all this evil has come upon us, and we have not entreated the face of **Yahuah** our Alahim, to turn back from our lawlessnesses, and to study Your truth. ₁₄Hence **Yahuah** has watched over the evil and has brought it upon us. For **Yahuah** our Alahim is obedient in all the works which He has done, but we have not obeyed His voice. ₁₅And now, **Yahuah** our Alahim, Who brought Your people out of the land of Mitsrim with a strong hand, and made Yourself a Name, as it is this yom – we have sinned, we have done lawless! ₁₆"**Yahuah**, according to all Your obedience, I pray, let Your displeasure and Your wrath be turned away from Your city Yerushalim, Your qodesh mountain. For, because of our sins, and because of the lawlessnesses of our fathers, Yerushalim and Your people have become a reproach to all those around us. ₁₇And now, our Alahim, hear the prayer of Your servant, and his supplications, and for the sake of **Yahuah** cause Your face to shine on Your qodesh place, which is laid waste. ₁₈"My Alahim, incline Your ear and hear. Open Your eyes and see our wastes, and the **city which is called by Your Name**. For we do not present our supplications before You because of our obedient actions, but because of Your great compassions. ₁₉"**Yahuah**, hear! O **Yahuah**, forgive! **Yahuah**, listen and act! Do not delay for Your own sake, my Alahim, for Your city and Your people are called by Your Name." ₂₀And while I was speaking, and praying, and admiting my sin and the sin of my people Yisharal, and presenting my supplication before **Yahuah** my Alahim for the qodesh mountain of my Alahim, ₂₁while I was still speaking in prayer, the man Gabrial, whom I had seen in the vision at the beginning, came close to me, in swift flight about the time of the evening offering. ₂₂And he made me understand, and talked with me, and said, "Danial, I have now come forth to make you wise concerning understanding. ₂₃At the beginning of your supplications a word went out, and I have come to make it known, for you are greatly appreciated. So consider the word and understand the vision: ₂₄ 70 weeks are decreed for your people and for your qodesh city, to put an end to the transgression, and to seal up sins, and to cover lawlessness, and to bring in everlasting obedience, and to seal up vision and prophet, and to anoint the Most Qodesh. ₂₅Know, then, and understand: **from the going forth of the command to restore and build Yerushalim until Messiah the Prince is 7 weeks and 62 weeks.** It shall be built again, with streets and a trench, but in times of affliction. ₂₆And after the 62 weeks Messiah shall be cut off and have nothing. And the people of a coming prince shall destroy the city and the qodesh place *[Titus, 70 CE]*. And the end of it is with a flood. And wastes are decreed, and **fighting until the end.** ₂₇And he shall confirm a covenant with many for 1 week. And in the middle of the week he shall put an end to slaughtering and meal offering. And on the wing of abomination he shall lay waste, even until the complete end and that which is decreed is poured out on the one who lays waste."

[My Judge is Alahim]

DANIAL

DANIAL - AKA: DANIEL

10

In the 3rd year of **Koresh** king of Persia a word was revealed to Danial, whose name was called Belteshatsar. And the word was true, and the conflict great. And he understood the word, and had understanding of the vision. ₂In those Yomim I, Danial, was mourning 3 weeks of Yomim. ₃I did not eat desirable food, and meat and wine did not come into my mouth, and I did not anoint myself at all, till the completion of 3 weeks of Yomim. ₄And on the 24th yom of the 1st month, while I was by the side of the great river, that is Kiddeqel, ₅then I lifted my eyes and looked and saw a certain man dressed in linen, whose loins were girded with gold of Uphaz! ₆And his body was like beryl, and his face like the appearance of lightning, and his eyes like torches of fire, and his arms and feet like polished bronze in appearance, and the sound of his words like the sound of a multitude. *[Likely a Seraphim, or burning one]* ₇And I, Danial, alone saw the vision, for the men who were with me did not see the vision, but a great trembling fell upon them, and they ran away to hide themselves. ₈So I was left alone when I saw this great vision, and no strength remained in me, for my dignity was destroyed in me, and I retained no strength. ₉But I heard the sound of his words. And while I heard the sound of his words I was stunned lying with my face to the ground. ₁₀And see, a hand touched me, and set me trembling on my knees and on the palms of my hands. ₁₁And he said to me, "Danial, man greatly appreciated, understand the words that I speak to you, and stand upright, for I have now been sent to you." And while he was speaking this word to me, I stood trembling. ₁₂And he said to me, "Do not fear, Danial, for from the 1st yom that you set your heart to understand and to humble yourself before your Alahim, your words were heard, and I have come because of your words. ₁₃But the head of the rule of Persia withstood me 21 Yomim. And see, **Mikal**, one of the chief heads, came to help me, for I had been left alone there with the kings of Persia. ₁₄And I have come to make you understand what is to befall your people in the latter Yomim. For the vision is yet for Yomim to come." ₁₅And when he had spoken such words to me, I turned my face toward the ground and kept silent. ₁₆And see, one who looked like the sons of men touched my lips, and I opened my mouth and spoke and said to him who stood before me, "My Aduni, because of the vision I have been seized with pains, and I have retained no strength. ₁₇So how was this servant of my Aduni able to speak with you, my Aduni? As for me, no strength remains in me now, nor is any breath left in me." ₁₈And again the one who looked like a man touched me and strengthened me. ₁₉And he said, "Do not fear, O man greatly appreciated! Peace be to you, be strong now, be strong!" So when he spoke to me I was strengthened, and said, "Let my Aduni speak, for you have strengthened me." ₂₀And he said, "Do you know why I have come to you? And now I return to fight with the head of Persia. And when I have left, see, the head of Greece shall come. ₂₁But let me declare to you what is written in the **Scripture of Truth**, and there is no one supporting me against these, except Mikal your head.

DANIAL - AKA: **DANIEL**

11

"And in the first year of Daryush the Mede, I myself stood up to support and protect him. ₂And now I declare the truth to you: See, 3 more kings are to arise in Persia, and the 4th is to become far richer than them all. And by his power, through his riches, he stirs up all against the rulership of Greece. ₃And a mighty king shall arise, and he shall rule with great authority, and do as he pleases. ₄But when he has arisen, his rule shall be broken up and divided toward the 4 winds of the shamayim, but not among his descendants nor according to his authority with which he ruled, because his rule shall be uprooted, even for others besides these. ₅And a king of the South shall become strong, along with one of his princes who gains power over him and shall rule – his rule being a great rule. ₆And at the end of years they shall join themselves together, and a daughter of the king of the South shall come to the king of the North to make an alliance. But she shall not retain the strength of her power, nor would he or his power stand. And she shall be given up, with those who brought her, and he who brought her forth, and he who supported her in those times. 7But from a branch of her roots one shall arise in his place, and he shall come into the defense and come into a stronghold of the king of the North, and shall act against them, and shall prevail, 8and also their mighty ones, with their princes and their precious utensils of silver and gold he shall seize and bring to Mitsrim. And he shall stand more years than the king of the North. 9Then he shall enter the reign of the king of the South, but shall return to his own land. 10But his sons shall stir themselves up, and assemble a great army. And he shall certainly come and overflow and pass through, then return to his stronghold, and be stirred up. 11Then the king of the South shall be enraged and go out to fight with him, with the king of the North, who shall raise a large army. But the army shall be given into the hand of his enemy, 12and he shall capture the army, his heart being exalted. And he shall cause tens of thousands to fall, but not prevail. 13And the king of the North shall return and raise an army greater than the former, and certainly come at the end of some years with a great army and much supplies. 14And in those times many shall rise up against the king of the South, while some violent ones among your people exalt themselves to establish the vision, but they shall stumble. 15Then the king of the North shall come in and build a siege mound, and capture a city of strongholds. And the arms of the South shall not stand, nor his choice people, for there is no strength to stand. 16So his opponent shall do as he pleases – with no one standing against him – and stand in the Marvelous Land with destruction in his hand. 17And he shall set his face to enter with the strength of his entire rule, and make an alliance with him. And he shall do so, and give him the daughter of women to corrupt her. But she shall not stand, neither be for him. 18Then he shall turn his face to the coastlands and capture many. But a ruler shall bring the reproach against them to an end. And with the reproach removed, he shall turn back on him. 19Then he shall turn his face toward the fortresses of his own land, but shall stumble and fall, and not be found. 20And in his place one shall stand up who imposes taxes on the adorned *city* of the rule, but within a few Yomim he is destroyed, but not in wrath or in battle. 21And in his place shall arise a despised one, to whom they shall not give the excellency of the rule. But he shall come in peaceably, and seize the rule by flatteries. 22And the arms of the flood shall be swept away from before him and be broken, and also the prince of the covenant. 23And after they joined him, he shall work deceit, and shall come up and become strong with a small nation. 24He shall enter peaceably, even into the richest places of the province, and do what his fathers have not done, nor his forefathers: distribute among them plunder and spoil and supplies, and devise his plots against the fortresses, but only for a time. 25And he shall stir up his power and his heart against the king of the South with a great army, and the king of the South shall be stirred up to battle with a very great and mighty army, but not stand, for they shall devise plots against him. 26And those who have been eating his food shall destroy him, and his army be swept away, and many fall down slain. 27And both these kings' hearts are to do evil, and speak lies at the same table, but not prosper, for the end is still for an appointed time. 28Then he shall return to his land with much supplies, and his heart be against the qodesh Covenant. And he shall act, and shall return to his land. 29At the appointed time he shall return and go toward the south, but it shall not be like the former or the latter. 30For ships from Kittim shall come against him, and he shall lose heart, and shall return in rage against the qodesh Covenant, and shall act, and shall return and consider those who forsake the qodesh Covenant. 31And strong ones shall arise from him and profane the qodesh place, the citadel, and shall take away that which is continual, and set up the abomination that lays waste. 32And by flatteries he shall profane those who do lawless against the Covenant, but the people who know their Alahim shall be strong, and shall act. 33And those of the people who have insight shall give understanding to many. And they shall stumble by sword and flame, by captivity and plundering, for Yomim. 34And when they stumble, they shall be helped, a little help, but many shall join them, by flatteries. 35And some of those who have insight shall stumble, to refine them, and to cleanse them, and to make them white, until the time of the end, for it is still for an appointed time. 36And the king shall do as he pleases, and exalt himself and show himself to be great above every mighty one, and speak incredible matters against the Al of mighty ones, and shall prosper until the wrath has been accomplished – for what has been decreed shall be done – 37and have **no regard** for the **mighty ones of his fathers** nor for the **desire of women**, nor have regard for any mighty one, but exalt himself above them all. 38But in his place he shall give esteem to a mighty one of fortresses. And to a mighty one which his fathers did not know he shall give esteem with gold and silver, with precious stones and costly gifts. 39And he shall act against the strongest fortresses with a foreign mighty one, which he shall acknowledge. He shall increase in esteem and cause them to rule over many, and divide the land for gain. 40At the time of the end the king of the South shall push at him, and the king of the North rush against him like a whirlwind, with chariots, and with horsemen, and with many ships. And he shall enter the lands, and shall overflow and pass over, 41and shall enter the Marvelous Land, and many shall stumble, but these escape from his hand: Adum, and Muab, and the chief of the sons of Ammon. 42And he shall stretch out his hand against the lands, and the land of Mitsrim shall not escape. 43And he shall rule over the treasures of gold and silver, and over all the riches of Mitsrim, and Libyans and Kushites shall be at his steps. 44Then reports from the east and the north shall disturb him, and he shall go out with great wrath to destroy and put many under the ban, 45 and he shall pitch the tents of his palace between the yamim and the marvelous qodesh mountain, but shall come to his end with none to help him.

DANIAL

DANIAL - AKA: DANIEL

12 "Now at that time Mikal shall stand up, the great head who is standing over the sons of your people. And there shall be a **time of distress**, such as never was since there was a nation, until that time. And at that time your people shall be delivered, every one who is found written in the book, 2and many of those who sleep in the dust of the arets wake up, some to everlasting life, and some to reproaches, everlasting abhorrence. 3**And those who have insight shall shine like the brightness of space, and those who lead many to obedience like the stars forever and ever.** 4But you, Danial, hide the words, and seal the book until the time of the end. Many shall diligently search and knowledge shall increase." 5Then I, Danial, looked and saw 2 others standing, one on this bank of the river and the other on that bank. 6And one said to the man dressed in linen, who was above the mayim of the river, "How long until the end of these wonders?" 7And I heard the man dressed in linen, who was above the mayim of the river, and he held up his right hand and his left hand to the shamayim, and swore by Him who lives forever, that it would be for a time, times, and half a time. And when they have ended scattering the power of the qodesh people, then all these shall be completed. 8And I heard, but I did not understand, so I said, "My Aduni, what is the latter end of these *matters*?" 9And he said, "Go, Danial, for the words are hidden and sealed till the time of the end. 10Many shall be cleansed and made white, and refined. But the lawless shall do lawless – and none of the lawless shall understand, but those who have insight shall understand. ₁₁And from the time that which is continual is taken away, and the abomination that lays waste is set up, is 1,290 Yomim. ₁₂Blessed is he who is waiting earnestly, and comes to the 1,335 Yomim. ₁₃But you, go your way till the end. And rest, and arise to your lot at the end of the Yomim."

[My Messenger]

MALAKI

MALAKI —AKA: **MALACHI**

1 **The message of the Word of Yahuah to Yisharal by Mal'aki.** ₂"I have loved you," said **Yahuah**. "But you asked, 'In what way have You loved us?' "Was not Esu Yaqub's brother?" says **Yahuah**. "And I love Yaqub, ₃but I have hated Esu, and have laid waste his mountains and his inheritance for the monsters of the wilderness." ₄If Adum says, "We have been beaten down, let us return and build the ruins," **Yahuah** Tsabauth said thus: "Let them build, but I tear down. And they shall be called 'Border of Wickedness', and the people against whom **Yahuah** is enraged forever. ₅And your eyes shall see, and you shall say, 'Great is **Yahuah** beyond the border of Yisharal!' ₆A son esteems his father, and a servant his Aduni. And if I am the Father, where is My esteem? And if I am a Aduni, where is My respect? said **Yahuah** Tsabauth to you priests who loathe My Name. But you asked, **'In what way have we loathed Your Name?'** ₇You are presenting corrupt food on My altar. But you asked, 'In what way have we corrupted You?' Because you say, 'The table of **Yahuah** is scornful.' ₈And when you present the blind as a slaughtering, is it not evil? And when you present the lame and sick, is it not evil? Bring it then to your governor! Would he be pleased with you? Would he accept you favorably?" said **Yahuah** Tsabauth. ₉"And now, entreat the face of Al to show favor to us. This has been done by your hands. Would He show favor to you?" said **Yahuah** Tsabauth. ₁₀"Who among you who would shut the doors, so that you would not kindle fire on My altar for nothing? I have no pleasure in you," said **Yahuah** Tsabauth, "Nor do I accept an offering from your hands. ₁₁For from the rising of the sun, even to its going down, My Name is great among Guyim. And in every place incense is presented to My Name, and a clean offering. For My Name is great among Guyim," said **Yahuah** Tsabauth. ₁₂"But you are profaning Me, in that you say, 'The table of **Yahuah** is scornful, and its fruit, its food, is wretched.' ₁₃And you said, 'Oh, what weariness!' and you sneered at it," said **Yahuah** Tsabauth. "And you brought in plunder, and the lame, and the sick – thus you have brought in the offering! Should I accept this from your hand?" said **Yahuah**. ₁₄"But cursed be the deceiver who has a male in his flock, and makes a vow, but is slaughtering to **Yahuah** what is imperfect. For I am a great King," said **Yahuah** Tsabauth, "and My Name is respected among Guyim.

MALAKI —AKA: **MALACHI**

2 "And now, priests, this command is for you. ₂If you do not hear, and if you do not take it to heart, to give esteem to My Name," said **Yahuah** Tsabauth, "I shall send a curse upon you, and I shall curse your blessings. And indeed, I have cursed them, because you do not take it to heart. ₃See, I shall rebuke your seed, and scatter rubbish before your faces, the rubbish of your festivals. And you shall be taken away with it. ₄And you shall know that I have sent this command to you, as being My Covenant with Lui," said **Yahuah** Tsabauth. ₅"My covenant with him was life and peace, and I gave them to him, to fear. And he respected Me, and stood in awe of My Name. ₆The **Turah of Truth**

was in his mouth, and disobedience was not found on his lips. He walked with Me in peace and straightness, and **turned many away from error**. 7For the lips of a priest should guard knowledge, and **they seek the Turah from his mouth, for he is the messenger of Yahuah Tsabauth.** 8But you, **you have turned from the Way, you have caused many to stumble in the Turah. You have corrupted the Covenant of Lui,**" said **Yahuah** Tsabauth. 9"And I also, I shall make you despised and low before all the people, because you are not guarding My ways, and are showing partiality in the Turah." 10Have we not all one Father? Did not one Al create us? Why do we act treacherously against one another, to profane the Covenant of the fathers? 11Yahudah has acted treacherously, and an abomination has been done in Yisharal and in Yerushalim, for Yahudah has profaned what is qodesh to **Yahuah** – which He had loved – and has married the daughter of a foreign mighty one. 12Let **Yahuah** cut off from the tents of Yaqub the man who does this – stirring up or answering, and bringing an offering to **Yahuah** Tsabauth! 13And this you have done a 2nd time: you cover the altar of **Yahuah** with tears, with weeping and crying, because He no longer regards the offering, nor receives it with pleasure from your hands. 14And you said, "Why?" Because **Yahuah** has been **witness between you and the ashah of your youth, against whom you have acted treacherously**, though she is your companion and the ashah of your covenant. 15And did He not make **one**? And He had the remnant of the Ruach? And what is the one *alone*? He seeks a seed of Alahim. So you shall guard your ruach, and let none act treacherously against the ashah of his youth. 16"**For I hate divorce,**" said **Yahuah** Alahim of Yisharal, "and the one who covers his garment with cruelty," said **Yahuah** Tsabauth. "So you shall guard your Ruach, and do not act treacherously. 17You have wearied **Yahuah** with your words, and you have said, "In what way have we wearied Him?" In that you say, "Everyone who does **evil is good** in the eyes of **Yahuah**, and He is delighting in them," or, "Where is the Alahim of lawfulness?"

MALAKI —AKA: **MALACHI**

3 "See, I am sending My **messenger**, and he shall prepare the way before Me. Then suddenly Aduni you are seeking comes to His Hekal, even the **Messenger of the Covenant**, in whom you delight. See, He is coming," said **Yahuah** Tsabauth. 2"And who is able to bear the yom of His coming, and who is able to stand when He appears? For He is like the fire of a refiner, and like the soap of a Launderer. 3And He shall sit as a refiner and a cleanser of silver. And He shall cleanse the sons of Lui, and refine them as gold and silver, and they shall belong to **Yahuah**, bringing near an offering in obedience. 4Then shall the offering of Yahudah and Yerushalim be pleasant to **Yahuah**, as in the Yomim of old, as in former years. 5And I shall draw near to you for lawfulness. And I shall be a swift witness against the practicers of witchcraft, and against adulterers, and against them that swear to falsehood, and against those who oppress the wage earner in his wages and widows and the fatherless, and those who turn away a traveller and do not fear Me," said **Yahuah** Tsabauth. 6"For I am **Yahuah**, I change not, and you, O sons of Yaqub, shall not come to an end. 7From the Yomim of your fathers you have turned aside from My laws and did not guard them. Turn back to Me, and I shall turn back to you," said **Yahuah** Tsabauth. But you said, 'In what shall we turn back?' 8Would a man rob Alahim? Yet you are robbing Me! But you said, 'In what have we robbed You?' In the tithe and the offering! 9You have cursed Me with a curse, for you are robbing Me, this nation, all of it! 10Bring all the tithes into the storehouse, and let there be food in My house. And please examine Me in this," said **Yahuah** Tsabauth, "whether I do not open for you the windows of the shamayim, and shall pour out for you boundless blessing! 11And I shall rebuke the devourer for you, so that it does not destroy the fruit of your ground, nor does the vine fail to bear fruit for you in the field," said **Yahuah** Tsabauth. 12"And all Guyim shall call you blessed, for you shall be a land of delight," said **Yahuah** Tsabauth. 13"Your words have been harsh against Me," said **Yahuah**, "but you have said, 'What have we spoken against You?' 14You have said, 'It is worthless to serve Alahim. And what did we gain when we guarded His charge, and when we walked as mourners before **Yahuah** Tsabauth? 15And now we are calling the proud blessed – not only are the doers of lawlessness built up, but they also test Alahim and escape.' " 16**Then shall those who fear Yahuah speak to one another**, and **Yahuah** listen and **hear**, and a **book of remembrance** be written before Him, **of those who fear Yahuah, and those who think upon His Name.** 17And they shall be **Mine**," said **Yahuah** Tsabauth, "on the yom that I prepare a **treasured possession**. And I shall spare them as a man spares his own son who serves him. 18Then you shall again see the *difference* between the obedient and the lawless, between **one who serves** Alahim and **one who does not serve** Him.

[My Messenger]

MALAKI

MALAKI —AKA: **MALACHI**

4 "For look, the yom shall come, burning like a furnace, and all the proud, and every lawless ones shall be stubble. And the yom that shall come shall burn them up," said **Yahuah** Tsabauth, "which leaves to them neither root nor branch. 2But to you who fear My Name the **Servant of Obedience** shall arise with healing in His wings. And you shall go out and leap for joy like calves from the stall. 3And you shall trample the lawless oness, for they shall be ashes under the soles of your feet on the yom that I do this," said **Yahuah** Tsabauth. 4"**Remember the Turah of Mushah**, My servant, which I commanded him in Koreb for all Yisharal – laws and directives. 5See, I am sending you **Aliyah** the Prophet before the coming of the great and awesome yom of **Yahuah**. 6And he shall turn the hearts of the fathers to the children, and the hearts of the children to their fathers, **lest I come and smite the arets with utter destruction.**"

INTRODUCTION TO THE NATSARIM WRITINGS

How to prepare for the end is explained here very clearly. Note that the preparation for the return of Yahusha at the time of the **Day of Yahuah** is preceded by the warning given at Malaki 4 *to remember the Turah of Mushah*. Specifically, this is the 10 Words of His Covenant.

When these Commands are obeyed and lived by Yahusha's Natsarim, we are accused of being legalists, as if legalism is heresy. Good is called evil, and evil is called good. Everyone should strive to be lawful, not lawless.

BYNV HEBREW ROOTS DICTIONARY OF CRITICAL WORDS

NATSARIM WRITINGS

The Natsarim Writings in this version are arranged in an order that better presents Yahusha as a **Turah Teacher**, in fact, the LIVING TURAH: the Word of life. Turah being the Light of the world, the **Living Word** of Yahuah, was previously "with" His people. Yahuah is doing a new thing: now the Ruach of Yahuah has come to dwell "in" His people. His mind, or Turah, is **alive** in us who **obey** His Word. "In the beginning" [**BARASHITH**] is announced a *second time*, since the Natsarim Writings reflect the Light, and announce the coming of the True Light. His first-followers warn us of a coming "falling-away" from the belief. There is also a hint in Shaul's writings of a future standing-away, or *apostasia*, which occurs in the last days. The Natsarim of today are *standing away* from the malicious teachers, and the strongholds they have imprisoned so many minds within for centuries. Yahusha's first-followers were trained in Turah observance from their childhood, but in Yahusha they met the living, breathing Turah, the Instructor Himself. Turah means instruction, and Turah instructs us in how to LOVE Yahuah, and our neighbor. Yahusha's living obedience to the Living Words is our best guide to follow Him, and walk as He walked. The traditional mindset repels obedience, so hopefully by this new arrangement of these memoirs, new readers will first be warned against "falling away" from the Turah. The first followers were servants, and they want to teach you many things traditional teachers want you to disregard. Open your heart, and listen to their words. They are words of love. The author of the "book of John" does not give his name directly, only indirectly, inferred from the phrase "the pupil whom Yahusha loved." He wrote this in his later years, but in the account he provides us, his identity happens to be the young brother of Miryam and Martha, whom Yahusha raised from the dead. You will see this to be true as you read it carefully to the end of the account. So what is his name? It happens to be Alazar *[Alahim helps]* also commonly called "Lazarus." Several of the Natsarim had 2 or even 3 names. Since the rulers were seeking to kill Alazar as well as Yahusha, it is possible he began to use one of his other names as an alternate, in order to remain anonymous to their plot. This is only a theory of the editorial staff. The palaeo-Hebrew you will see in the text represents the authentic letters which spell the Name "Yahusha."

Yahusha's Name means ***"I am your Deliverer."***

TRANSLITERATIONS

	6,823 YAHUAH	216 YAHUSHA	2 YAHUSHUA	1 Y'SHUA
HEBREW	ⱯYⱯ⁊	OWYⱯ⁊	OYWYⱯ⁊	OYW⁊
ARAMAIC	יהוה	יהושׁע	יהושׁוע	ישׁוע
GREEK	IAOUE	IHSOUS		
LATIN	IEHOUAH	IESU		

AT HEBREWS 4 AND ACTS 7 THE SAME GREEK LETTERING IS USED
FOR "JOSHUA" AND "JESUS" - IHSOUS
THIS IS CONFIRMATION BOTH WERE CALLED YAHUSHA IN HEBREW
TORAH INSTITUTE

WHAT'S MISSING?

Why is Yahusha's Spirit not received by many people?
The lack of obedience prevents people from receiving Him.
Acts 5:32 explains it – The Spirit is ONLY given to those who obey Him.

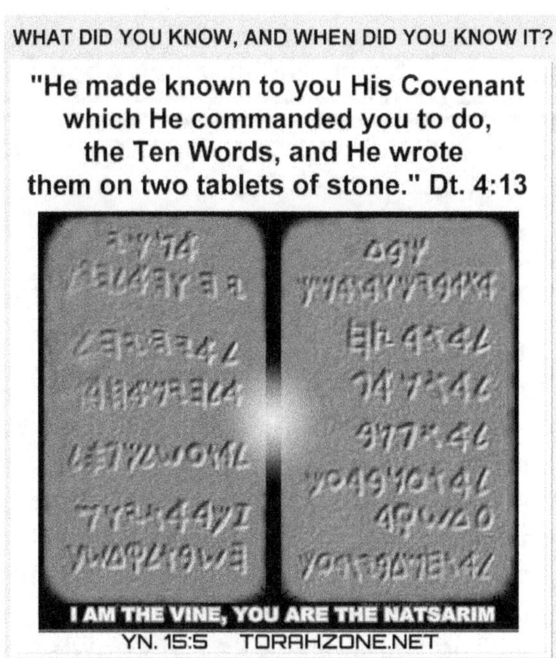

OBEDIENCE

That's what's missing.

People are trained to *disobey*, and **they do not know** the NAME of the One they are told they serve. It's destroyed.

*Yahusha's Spirit is only given to those who **obey** Him.*

Acts 5:32 explains to us the simple reason some people can't receive the Ruach ha Qodesh (indwelling Spirit of Yahusha to assist us). The reason is this*: **they have not yet obeyed His Commandments,** because *their teachers* have misled them.

People have been taught the Commandments were "done away," but Yahusha's blood purchased us, ended animal blood offerings, and the old priesthood. He did not destroy His Torah. Our belief is perfected by obedience, and it is obedience that gives living evidence of our belief.

1 Korinthians 19:27-30 explains to the former pagans about the gifts of Yahusha's *Spirit*, and that there are different gifts among all the members of the body.

Paul's writings are very difficult to understand for the untaught and immature, causing divisiveness in the body. They argue and bite.

Galatians 5:14-26 warns us about the biting, provoking, and envying we see increasing everywhere online, another indication that Yahusha is near and separating His sheep from His goats. We

need to be one of His sheep, and do what He commissioned us to
do, teach all nations the Name and that they **obey** everything He
commanded us to obey. (Mt. 28:19-20)
Paul asked the Galatians, *have I now become your enemy, having
told you the Truth?* (Galatians 4).
Always teach, correct, and train using Scripture - with humbleness,
not haughtiness. (2 Tim. 4)
Snatch some from the fire before the time runs out to help them.

THE KEY OF KNOWLEDGE
Psalm 118:26 has a phrase,
    "Blessed is the One coming in the Name of YAHUAH."
The Hebrew transliteration of this is shown written at the top of this
page. As Yahusha was riding on a young donkey into the city a few
days prior to His death, the crowds were shouting this.
Because **uttering the Name aloud** was forbidden, the Pharisees
ordered Yahusha to correct His followers and make them *stop
saying this Name.* The Name is the **key of knowledge** they had
withheld from those they taught.
    The builders rejected the *keystone.*

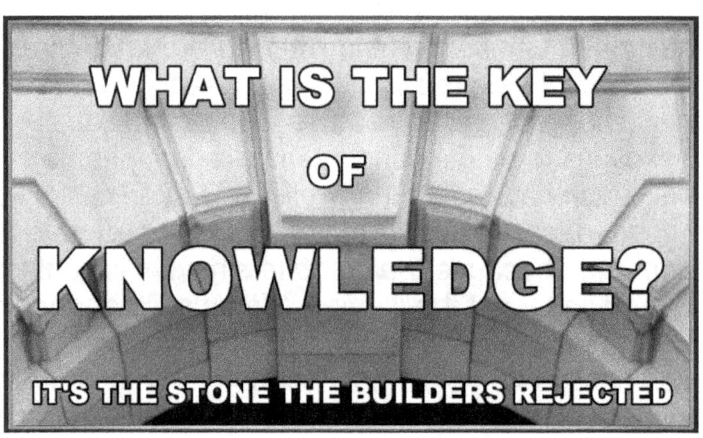

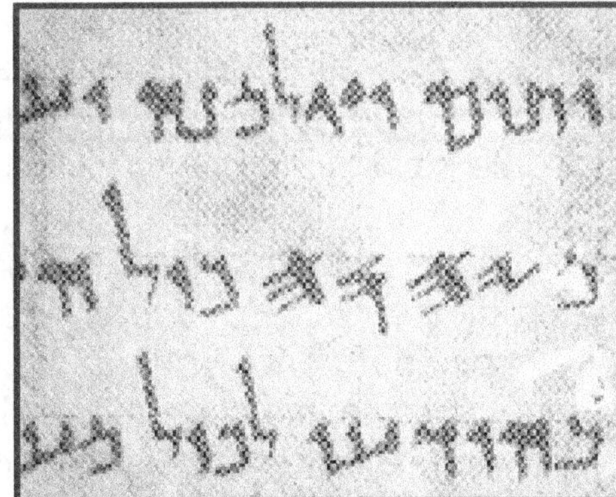

SOME PHOTOS LINKED TO WEB PAGES

NASB - PRINCIPLES OF TRANSLATION

The Proper Name of God in the Old Testament: In the Scriptures, the name of God is most significant and understandably so. It is inconceivable to think of spiritual matters without a proper designation for the Supreme Deity. Thus the most common name for deity is God, a translation of the Hebrew *Elohim*. The normal word for Master is Lord, a rendering of *Adonai*. There is yet another name which is particularly assigned to God as His special or proper name, that is, the four letters YHWH (Exodus 3:14 and Isaiah 42:8). This name has not been pronounced by the Jews because of reverence for the great sacredness of the divine name. Therefore, it was consistently pronounced and translated LORD. The only exception to this translation of YHWH is when it occurs in immediate proximity to the word Lord, that is, *Adonai*. In that case it is regularly translated GOD in order to avoid confusion.

NIV - PREFACE

In regard to the divine name *YHWH*, commonly referred to as the *Tetragrammaton*, the translators adopted the device used in most English versions of rendering that name as "LORD" in capital letters to distinguish it from *Adonai*, another Hebrew word rendered "Lord," for which small letters are used. Wherever the two names stand together in the Old Testament as a compound name of God, they are rendered "Sovereign LORD."

Because for most readers today the phrases "the LORD of hosts" and "God of hosts" have little meaning, this version renders them "the LORD Almighty" and "God Almighty." These renderings convey the sense of the Hebrew, namely, "he who is sovereign over all the 'hosts' (powers) in heaven and on earth, especially over the 'hosts' (armies) of Israel." For readers unacquainted with Hebrew this does not make clear the distinction between *Sabaoth* ("hosts" or "Almighty") and *Shaddai* (which can also be translated "Almighty"), but the latter occurs infrequently and is always footnoted. When *Adonai* and *YHWH Sabaoth* occur together, they are rendered "the Lord, the LORD Almighty."

As for other proper nouns, the familiar spellings of the King James Version are generally retained.

Examining the context or Psalm 118:26, we read of a STONE the builders rejected. The metaphors STONE and KEY refer to the Name the teachers still refuse to receive. Since the translators of today still withhold the Name, and would never consider obeying the Commandments, you've been trusting in the translations of men who did not possess the indwelling Spirit of Yahusha, and have been taught by others not having Him, for centuries. If they had Him, they would have **taught** you His true Name, to **obey** everything He Commanded, and walk as He walked.
You can not have His Spirit, **_and_** walk in lawlessness.

EARTH WILL BE BURNED FOR BREAKING THE EVERLASTING COVENANT

YashaYahu / Is. 24:1-6:
"See, Yahuah is making the arets empty and making it waste, and shall overturn its surface, and shall scatter abroad its inhabitants. And it shall be – as with the people so with the priest, as with the servant so with his Aduni, as with the female servant so with her mistress, as with the buyer so with the seller, as with the lender so with the borrower, as with the creditor so with the debtor; the arets is completely emptied and utterly plundered, for Yahuah has spoken this word. The arets shall mourn and wither, the world shall languish and wither, the haughty people of the arets shall languish. For the arets has been defiled under its inhabitants, because they have transgressed the Turoth, changed the law, broken the everlasting Covenant. Therefore a curse shall consume the arets, and those who dwell in it be punished. Therefore the inhabitants of the arets shall be burned, and few men shall be left."
If anyone claims *"I know Him,"* but they do not guard His Commandments, *they are a liar.*
(See 1 Yn. 2:4)

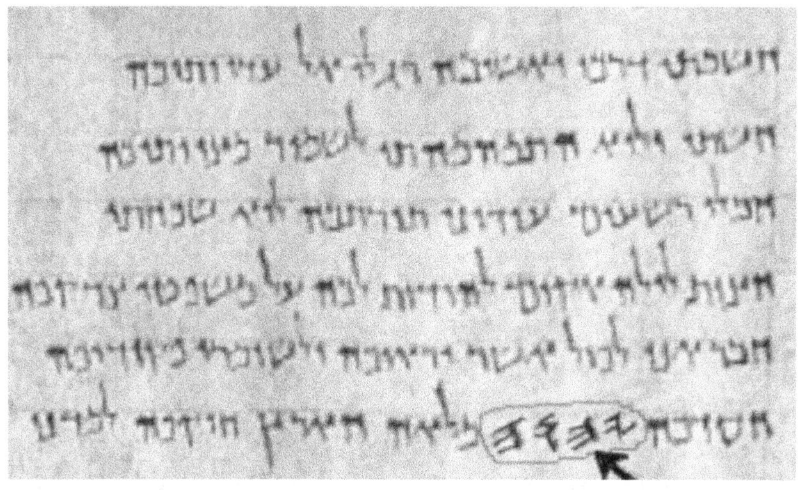

The Name **Yahuah** appears above in ancient Hebrew, with the surrounding text in Aramaic. The scribe would **stop** at the Name, and another would come to write the Name. As he would write, he would pause after each letter, and two sets of eyes would evaluate before proceeding to the next letter. The Aramaic script was readable to the post-Exilic Yahudim; that is why most of the text is written in Aramaic.

WE ARE IN THE LAST DAYS

Pastors confuse and trick to get you to stay away from reading the book of Revelation for a good reason. Many now read and understand, as Danial 12 says they will in the last days. Revelation 22:11-15 is proof that we have been taught to disobey by liars:
"He who does lawlessness, let him do more lawlessness; he who is filthy, let him be more filthy; he who is obedient, let him be more obedient; he who is qodesh, let him be more qodesh. And see, I am coming speedily, and My reward is with Me, to give to each
according to his work. I am the Alef and the Tau, The Beginning and the End, the First and the Last. Blessed are those doing His commands so that the authority shall be theirs to the tree of life, and to enter through the gates into the city. But outside are the dogs and those who enchant with drugs, and those who whore, and the murderers, and the idolaters, and all who love and do falsehood." (BYNV)
Another verse, Revelation 12:17, is impossible to miss for those who serve Yahusha, rather than trying to make *Him* do *their* will. *Notice what enrages the dragon:*
"And the dragon was enraged with the ashah, and he went to fight with the remnant of her seed, those guarding the Commands of Yahuah, and possessing the witness of Yahusha Mashiak."
Constantine changed the day of rest to his Sun deity, but Yahusha told us to pray our flight not be in winter, or on a Shabath.
See Mt. 24:20, a prophecy concerning the END OF DAYS, during the great distress.

Obedience is not in their wheelhouse.
When you obey, you receive HIM!
JOIN NATSARIMLIFE.COM

IS YAHUSHA A PHARISEE?

Yahusha is not a Pharisee, Sadducee, Essene, Qaraite, nor a Christianos. He said He is the Root, and His followers are the Natsarim (Yahukanon 15:5).
Yahusha is THE teacher, and the only exalted one (Rab). He is the ultimate authority.
The teaching authorities asked Him where He had received His authority to teach, and this indicates He was under the authority of no person or group. He is the King of Yisharal, Creator of all that is

seen and unseen, and Al Shaddai. His credentials are from everlasting (past) to everlasting (future). At Mt. 28:18 Yahusha said He possesses all authority in Shamayim and in arets, meaning what He says is what we do. All power rests in the hands of Al Shaddai.

How could He be a member of a humanly-organized sect? YashaYahu 45:7 is a text explaining that He creates light, darkness, peace, chaos, and is the Possessor of Shamayim and arets. He is about to surprise many who have been misled.

His ambassadors are here now (see 2 Korinthians 5:20).

GOD EL AL ALAH ALAHIM STORM IN LOUISVILLE...

WILL THE REAL HERETIC PLEASE STAND UP

SATANS SACRAMENTS REPLACED THE PLAN OF...

SHADOW OF THINGS TO COME - dragon thought to...

WHAT DENOMINATION ARE YOU

WATCH HUNDREDS OF TEACHING VIDEOS ON LEW WHITE YOUTUBE CHANNEL

YAHUSHA NAMED US NATSARIM

WHY IS MANKIND CONFUSED? REBELLION...

WHY I DO NOT USE THE NAME JESUS

WHAT THE DEVIL HATES

OPINION OF HABIT TRADITION HYPNOTIZES...

Thank you for presenting your remaining time in the flesh to Yahusha to serve Him, and becoming an *ambassador* of His coming reign. Our enemy is not flesh and blood, so please expect the resistance that will ensue. This book is intended to awaken the *many* spoken of in Danial 12, leading *many* to obedience prior to the coming of our Creator Yahusha.

I hope to see you at the marriage supper.

By Lew White
PHOTO LINKED TO AUTHOR'S PAGE

HALLELU YAH

BARUK HABA BASHEM YAHUAH

Order from anywhere to receive more of these books
Lew White – Amazon.com Author's Page

9 798847 612753